D0355403

# Beyond
# the
# Quantum

# BANTAM NEW AGE BOOKS

This important imprint includes books in a variety of fields and disciplines and deals with the search for meaning, growth and change. They are books that circumscribe our times and our future.

Ask your bookseller for the books you have missed.

METAMAGICAL THEMAS: QUESTING FOR THE ESSENCE OF MIND
    AND PATTERN by Douglas R. Hofstadter
MIND AND NATURE by Gregory Bateson
THE MIND'S I by Douglas R. Hofstadter and Daniel C. Dennett
NATURAL ESP: THE ESP CORE AND ITS RAW CHARACTERISTICS
    by Ingo Swann
THE NEW STORY OF SCIENCE by Robert M. Augros and
    George N. Stanciu
ON HUMAN NATURE by Edward O. Wilson
ORDER OUT OF CHAOS by Ilya Prigogine and Isabelle Stengers
ORIGINS: A SKEPTIC'S GUIDE TO THE CREATION OF LIFE ON
    EARTH by Robert Shapiro
PERFECT SYMMETRY by Heinz R. Pagels
PROSPERING WOMAN by Ruth Ross
SCIENCE, ORDER, AND CREATIVITY by David Bohm and
    F. David Peat
SHAMBHALA: THE SACRED PATH OF THE WARRIOR by
    Chogyam Trungpa
SPACE-TIME AND BEYOND (The New Edition) by Bob Toben and
    Fred Alan Wolf
STAYING SUPPLE by John Jerome
SUPERMIND by Barbara B. Brown
SYMPATHETIC VIBRATIONS: REFLECTIONS ON PHYSICS AS A
    WAY OF LIFE by K. C. Cole
SYNCHRONICITY: THE BRIDGE BETWEEN MATTER AND MIND
    by F. David Peat
THE TAO OF LEADERSHIP by John Heider
THE TAO OF PHYSICS (Revised Edition) by Fritjof Capra
TO HAVE OR TO BE? by Erich Fromm
THE TURNING POINT by Fritjof Capra
THE WAY OF THE SHAMAN: A GUIDE TO POWER AND HEALING
    by Michael Harner
ZEN AND THE ART OF MOTORCYCLE MAINTENANCE by
    Robert M. Pirsig

## About the Author

**Michael Talbot** began his journey "beyond the quantum" as a child in northern Michigan, where his family endured the frequent visits of a poltergeist. His curiosity about the paranormal increased as the poltergeist visited him at Michigan State and later, when he moved to New York City. His quest has led him to write frequently on the failure of scientific orthodoxy to explain this phenomenon. He is the author of *Mysticisim and the New Physics* and two novels, most recently *The Bog*.

# Beyond the Quantum

## MICHAEL TALBOT

BANTAM BOOKS
TORONTO · NEW YORK · LONDON · SYDNEY · AUCKLAND

BEYOND THE QUANTUM

*A Bantam Book / published by arrangement with
Macmillan Publishing Company*

PRINTING HISTORY

*Macmillan edition published January 1987*

*New Age and the accompanying figure design as well as the
statement "the search for meaning, growth and change" are
trademarks of Bantam Books.*

*Bantam edition / April 1988*

LIBRARY OF CONGRESS
Library of Congress Cataloging-in-Publication Data

Talbot, Michael, 1953–
  Beyond the quantum / Michael Talbot.
    p.    cm.
  Originally published: New York : Macmillan, c1986.
  Includes index.
  ISBN 0-553-34480-3
    1. Quantum theory.   2. Physics—Philosophy.   3. Science—
—Philosophy.   4. Reality.   I. Title.
QC174.12.T35 1988
530.1'2—dc19                                      87-30726
                                                      CIP

*Published simultaneously in the United States and Canada*

PRINTED IN THE UNITED STATES OF AMERICA

O      0  9  8  7  6  5  4  3  2  1

For Anna Valentine with much love
from her grandson.

Normal science does not aim at novelties of fact or theory and, when successful, finds none. New and unsuspected phenomena are, however, repeatedly uncovered by scientific research, and radical new theories have again and again been invented by scientists. History even suggests that the scientific enterprise has developed a uniquely powerful technique for producing surprises of this sort. If this characteristic of science is to be reconciled with what has already been said, then research under a paradigm must be a particularly effective way of inducing a paradigm change. That is what fundamental novelties of fact and theory do. Produced inadvertently by a game played under one set of rules, their assimilation requires the elaboration of another set. After they have become parts of science, the enterprise, at least of those specialists in whose particular field the novelties lie, is never quite the same again.

—THOMAS S. KUHN, *The Structure of Scientific Revolutions*

# CONTENTS

# 9

## Why Is Science Afraid of the Paranormal? 217

# Acknowledgments

It is difficult to acknowledge all of the people who (in one way or another) contributed to the writing of this book, but a few who deserve special mention include: Marcia Richards and Martha Visser for friendship and moral support; Rupert Sheldrake for reading pertinent sections of the book and offering comments and suggestions; Fred Alan Wolf and Alan Guth for fascinating conversation; Robert Butts for reading and offering comment on the Seth chapter; John Gliedman for generously granting me permission to quote from his various writings; Jim Gordon and Carol Dryer for their insights and guidance; and Charles Levine and Ed Novak for their gentle and conscientious editing.

Grateful acknowledgment is made to the following for permission to reprint previously published material from:

J. M. Dent & Sons Ltd, Publishers, London. *God and the New Physics* by Paul Davies. Copyright © 1983 by Paul Davies. Reprinted with permission of the publisher.

E. P. Dutton, New York. *Mind and Nature* by Gregory Bateson. Copyright © 1979 by Gregory Bateson. Reprinted with permission of the publisher.

John Gliedman, "Mind and Matter," *Science Digest* (March 1983), excerpts reprinted with permission of the author. "Beyond the Brain's Boundaries," *Science Digest* (June 1984), excerpts reprinted with permission of the author. "Turning Einstein Upside Down," *Science Digest* (October 1984), excerpts reprinted with permission of the author.

Harper & Row, New York. *Disturbing the Universe* by Freeman Dyson. Copyright © 1979 by Freeman Dyson. Reprinted with permission of the publisher. *Physics and Philosophy* by Werner Heisenberg. Copyright © 1958 by Werner Heisenberg. Reprinted by permission of the publisher. *Conjuring Up Philip* by Iris M. Owen with Margaret Sparrow. Copyright © 1976 by Iris M. Owen. Reprinted with permission of the publisher. *Recollections of Death* by Michael B. Sabom. Copyright ©

1982 by Michael B. Sabom. Reprinted with permission of the publisher.

Macmillan Publishing Company, New York. *Contrasts* by Wiktor Osiatyński. Copyright © 1984 by Ewa Weydyłło-Woźniak. Reprinted by permission of the publisher. *The Wonder of Being Human* by Sir John Carew Eccles and Daniel N. Robinson. Copyright © 1984 by The Free Press, a division of Macmillan, Inc. Reprinted with permission of the publisher.

*New Realities* Magazine, San Francisco. "Rupert Sheldrake, Ph.D.," by Daniel Drasin, *New Realities* (December 1983). Copyright © 1983 by Daniel Drasin. Reprinted with permission of the publisher.

New Science Library, A Division of Shambhala Publications, Inc., Boston, Massachusetts. "The Physicist and the Mystic—Is a Dialogue between them Possible?" by David Bohm and Renee Weber in *The Holographic Paradigm and Other Paradoxes* by Ken Wilbur (Boston, Massachusetts: New Science Library, 1982), pp. 35–43. Reprinted with permission of the publisher.

*New Scientist*, London. "What Is It Like To Be Me?" by Daniel C. Dennett, *New Scientist* (September 24, 1981), pp. 805–807. Reprinted with permission of the publisher. "Review: A New Science of Life," by Brian Goodwin. *New Scientist* (July 16, 1981), p. 164. Reprinted with permission of the publisher. "Making a Monkey of Shakespeare," by David Osselton, *New Scientist* 104, no. 1,428 (November 1, 1984), p. 39. Reprinted with permission of the publisher.

*The New York Times*, New York. "Quantum Theory: Disturbing Questions Remain Unresolved," by Malcolm W. Brown, *The New York Times*, February 11, 1986, p. C3. Copyright © 1986 by The New York Times Company. Reprinted with permission.

*Omni* Magazine, New York. "Out-of-Body Survey," by Tom Kovach. *Omni* 4, no. 11 (August 1982): p. 94. "Interview with Ilya Prigogine," by Robert B. Tucker. *Omni* 8, no. 5 (May 1983) pp. 85–92 and 120–121. "Interview with Brian Josephson," by John Gleidman. *Omni* 4, no. 10 (July 1982), p. 88.

Prentice-Hall, Inc., Englewood Cliffs, N.J. *The Seth Material* by Jane Roberts (Englewood Cliffs, NJ: Prentice-Hall, Inc., 1970). *Seth Speaks* by Jane Roberts (Englewood Cliffs, NJ: Prentice-Hall, Inc., 1972). *The "Unknown" Reality* by Jane Roberts (Englewood Cliffs, NJ: Prentice-Hall, Inc., 1977). Reprinted with permission of the publisher.

Science, Washington, D.C. "Is Your Brain Really Necessary?" by Roger Lewin. *Science* 210 (December 12, 1980): pp. 1232–1234. Copyright © by the American Association for the Advancement of Science. Reprinted with permission of the publisher. "Quantum Mechanics

Passes Another Test" by Arthur Robinson. *Science* 217 (July 10, 1982): pp. 435–436. Copyright © by the American Association for the Advancement of Science. Reprinted with permission of the publisher.

*Science 84*, Washington, D.C. "How Did Language Begin?" by Ann Finkbeiner. *Science 84* (May, 1984), p. 26. Reprinted with permission of the publisher.

*Scientific American*, New York. "The Mind-Body Problem," by Jerry A. Fodor. *Scientific American* (January 1981). Reprinted with permission of the publisher.

The University of Chicago Press, Chicago, Illinois. *The Structure of Scientific Revolutions* by Thomas S. Kuhn. Copyright © 1970 by Thomas S. Kuhn. Reprinted with permission of the publisher.

*The Washington Post*, Washington, D.C., "Sheldrake the Magician," by Michael Kernan, June 9, 1983. Reprinted with permission of the publisher.

# INTRODUCTION

In 1982, an extraordinary experiment was performed. A research team composed of physicists Alain Aspect, Jean Dalibard, and Gérard Roger at the Institute of Theoretical and Applied Optics in Paris made what may prove to be one of the most significant discoveries of the century. Their findings brought to a close not only one of the longest running debates in the history of science, but cast grave doubts on some of our most basic assumptions about what we call reality.

Aspect's team brilliantly confirmed quantum theory, the study of matter at the subatomic level. This came as no surprise to most scientists. For over sixty years now, quantum theory has so successfully predicted and described physical phenomena that few doubted it would ultimately be vindicated. What *is* surprising is that Aspect's experiment has been almost completely ignored by the media and the general public, not because its implications are unimportant but because they are so profound they seem more science fiction than science fact.

In short, Aspect's experiment proved one of the following two possibilities: Either objective reality does not exist and it is meaningless for us to speak of things or objects as having any reality above and beyond the mind of an observer, *or* faster-than-light communication with the future and the past is possible. On these two points the conclusions of the Aspect experiment are unequivocal. These are *not* hypothetical assertions. At least one of the above two options must now be accepted as fact.

Perhaps the most startling feature of the Aspect experiment is that such a historic event took place with so little notice. Immediately following the experiment, many physicists had remarkably little to say about Aspect's dramatic disclosure. Between 1982 and 1985, a few articles appeared in various scientific journals praising the work of the French team, but assessed it ultimately only with brief and tantalizingly vague sentences like "lead(s) to realities beyond our common experience"[1] and "indicate(s) that we must be prepared to consider radically new views of reality."[2]

In a BBC radio program several months after Aspect published his results, British theoretical physicist Paul Davies asked a number of his distinguished colleagues for their reactions and received equally unsubstantive replies. Several expressed no surprise and said that they had been expecting such results for years. Others begrudgingly conceded that perhaps some signals could travel faster than light, but argued that there still must be some undiscovered mechanism that prevents such signals from being sent in a controlled way. But as Davies noted in a written account of the program, once again the reality issue "was left vague."[3]

Finally, at a conference on "New Techniques and Ideas in Quantum Measurement Theory," held in New York in January 1986, a few physicists came forward with the first significant proposals about what the Aspect experiment may mean for the future of science. As we will see, their assertions are as profound as Aspect's findings, yet scientists still do not know what to make of it all.

Why has such an important event—the final proof that reality as we know it does not exist at the subatomic level—been greeted with so much silence and stupefaction? Part of the *real* reason is that the view of reality offered by quantum theory, and now Aspect's findings, assaults simple common sense. Another reason, I suspect, is that as long as quantum theory had not yet received final confirmation, many physicists were content to focus on its more functional aspects and refrain from commenting on its more disturbing philosophical implications.

The Aspect experiment is not the only recent scientific development with profound metaphysical implications. In

the past four or five years a surprising number of distinguished scientists have advanced theories in which they
assert that within some of our most current scientific
discoveries we are beginning to find at least partial answers
to some of the great mystical questions of all time. Can the
consciousness survive apart from the body? Do we receive
information only through our known senses, or are we each
also hooked into a collective part of our being? Is the universe an accident, or is it the product of intelligent design?
And what is the ultimate relationship between mind and
reality?

It should be noted that many of these views are highly
controversial, and it would be safe to say that a significant
number of scientists will rebel at some of the ideas reported
here. However, it is also worth mentioning that the advancement of science has often depended on the introduc-
tion of controversial ideas initially supported by only a few
brave thinkers and that, at the very least, the speculations
offered by many of the scientists in this book attempt to cut
through the "vagueness" that so often surrounds findings as
disconcerting and challenging as the results of the Aspect
experiment. The authors of many of these recent speculations are often as eminent in their fields, and widely re-
spected for other scientific contributions, as their current
offerings are provocative.

Here are a few of the ideas that will be discussed:

- In 1981, Cambridge biologist Rupert Sheldrake published a theory proposing that the form and natural intelligence of animals and even human beings is molded
and influenced by a ghostly new type of field that is able
to communicate across both space and time.
- The same year, David Bohm, a theoretical physicist at
the University of London and the author of one of the
standard textbooks on quantum theory, proposed that
the workings of the subatomic world only make sense if

we assume the existence of other more complex dimensions beyond our own.

· In 1983, Sir Fred Hoyle, the founder of the Cambridge Institute of Theoretical Astronomy and the man responsible for our current understanding of the origin of all heavy elements in the universe, proposed that within the laws of physics there is not only mathematical evidence that the universe was designed by some sort of cosmic intelligence, but that intelligence is unfathomably old, billions of years older than the age of the known universe.

· And in 1984, Nobel Prize–winning neurophysiologist Sir John Eccles announced the discovery of what he believes to be biochemical evidence supporting the existence of the human soul.

These are only a few of the recent, thought-provoking revelations that will be covered in this book. In addition to their intriguing and controversial nature, I would also like to submit that they have several other aspects in common. First, they underscore once again the continued inroads that both quantum physics and science in general are making into issues previously considered exclusively the province of the mystical.

In this regard I would like to say at the outset that what I mean by mystical is all those propositions which convention has always ascribed to the supernatural but which may really be only natural phenomena not yet understood. In other words, it is not my purpose to incorporate into science an element of pure faith, only to suggest that the metaphysics of today may be the physics of tomorrow. Thus, although the speculations offered in this book may at times become rather wide ranging, it is important to remember that they cannot be considered fact until proven by the tools and experimental methods of science.

The second and most important aspect the disclosures in

this book have in common is that many suggest that there are things not yet known in science—important laws of physics still waiting to be discovered. On this matter there are two schools of thought. The first, held by many physicists, is that we have just about figured out all there is to figure out about the basic laws of physics. This point of view is evidenced by the fact that there is once again a murmuring afoot in scientific circles that we are close to understanding nature, that we are just about to understand all there is to know about the forces that brought both the universe and life as we know it into being. This optimism is due in large part to the fact that in the past two decades, physicists have made considerable headway in developing a unified understanding of the four known forces of nature—gravitation, electromagnetism, the strong nuclear force, and the weak nuclear force.

The second school of thought holds that though our current achievements may be impressive, we are nowhere near understanding all of the forces responsible for bringing our universe into being. It is the view of this school that there are still many puzzling things going on in our world that are real and have not yet been adequately explained by science.

In arguing against the first school one need merely look at the history of science as a case in point. Time and again throughout the course of human discovery, otherwise great thinkers have in moments of careless rumination made the same prediction, invariably with seriously embarrassing results. The eminent British physicist Lord Kelvin looked back on the prodigious scientific accomplishments of the nineteenth century and boasted that all future work in physics would amount to nothing more than "adding a few decimal places to results already obtained." On the horizon he noted there were only "two small dark clouds." The two small dark clouds were, of course, Einstein's theory of special relativity, and quantum theory. The folly of Lord Kelvin's remark is now obvious.

The three most common mistakes made by scientists that lead to such errors I call the three ugly stepsisters of science. The first, the compulsion of each generation of scientists to believe that they are on the very brink of finding out all there is to find out, is the Edge of the Map Syndrome. It seems an almost biological need for the human race, like the ancient mariners, to believe that beyond the boundary of human knowledge there exists only a void. But since nature abhors a vacuum, I suspect that we will always find the void is not a void at all, but just new territory to be mapped.

The second is the Limit Syndrome—the tendency to believe that if a rule or limit applies in a great number of cases it must therefore apply in all cases. And the third is a category of things I call Ptolemaic Conceits after Ptolemy, the second-century Alexandrian astronomer who developed a predictive model of the universe with Earth at its center. Keeping this tradition, Ptolemaic Conceits are those assumptions that may seem to make a lot of sense from a purely human perspective, but would probably seem the height of rudeness to any sentient being who is not a human. Keep these three ugly sisters in mind for, as we will see in coming chapters, they have reared their heads often throughout the history of science.

I belong to the second school of thought, the one that believes that there are great physics discoveries still to come, and I have a reason for my bias. As a child, the house in which I grew up became the center of a pronounced poltergeist haunting.* The phenomenon first manifested itself when I was about six years old in occasional, inexplicable showers of gravel raining down on our roof at night. When my father investigated, the showers invariably stopped, but at times they became so vigorous that he had to sweep the gravel off in the morning. At first my parents believed there

---

* The word *poltergeist* comes from a German expression meaning "noisy ghost" and is usually defined as a disembodied spirit that manifests in the form of rappings and other noisy disturbances.

was nothing paranormal about the occurrences and were simply at a loss for an explanation. Our home was rather isolated in the woods of the Michigan countryside, and there was little chance that neighbors or passers-by might be responsible for so regular an occurrence. Nonetheless, on one occasion when I went walking in the evening hours with some friends and gravel rained down on top of our heads, my father still remained convinced that the phenomenon was due to some elusive prankster and spent several hours unsuccessfully scanning the trees with a flashlight.

It wasn't until the phenomenon moved inside our house that we began to more fully comprehend its real nature. It stomped and rattled and, on less frequent occasions, pelted me with small objects. Small polished stones and bits of broken glass with edges worn as if they had been tumbled ceaselessly by some unknown ocean were its favorite projectiles. It also developed a marked fondness for throwing the vacuum cleaner around. If my mother happened to leave a room before she had finished vacuuming, we would quite regularly hear the distinctive clatter of the vacuum's hoses as it was picked up and then tossed back to the floor in another part of the room. Mercifully, the poltergeist never developed any interest in throwing the vacuum cleaner at us.

On occasion it also produced the most awesome crashing sounds, as if entire cupboards full of dishes had fallen and broken. But when we investigated we did not find the source of the noise. Once my parents were sitting in the living room when they heard all of the cupboards in the kitchen banging open and shut, the sound of dishes and canned goods falling out, the distinctive squeak of a Lazy Susan cupboard twirling rapidly around, and even the sound of the trash tipping over and tin cans rolling across the floor. But the moment they stood up the sound stopped and when they reached the kitchen they found nothing out of place.

Less frequently we actually saw objects move. I vividly recall watching a bottle of furniture polish slide quickly across a tabletop and topple onto the floor. On another occasion when I was with a friend, we opened the door to a room and no sooner had we done so when a lamp clicked on inside and a drinking glass flew out and broke against the hallway wall behind us. On examination we found that all the windows in the room were closed and locked, and there was, of course, no one inside.

In spite of the annoying aspects of such events my family became quite fascinated with what was happening around us. Indeed, we became so accustomed to the "presence" that, as children, if my two sisters and I were playing alone in the house and something invisible stomped up the stairs, as soon as we saw that it was not a prowler but only "it," we would simply return to our play.

Remarkably, it wasn't until I was an adolescent that I made my first attempt to contact the poltergeist. Late one night when I was standing in the kitchen I said aloud, "Okay, why don't you do something to show me that you're here?" When I made the remark I happened to be facing an open kitchen window—since our house was in the middle of the woods, we did not draw the curtains at night. No sooner had I mouthed the words when something invisible instantly began to pound on the glass, rapidly and with such force that I could not understand why the glass did not break. Taken off guard by the unexpected response, I panicked and screamed for the pounding to stop, and just as quickly as it had started, it stopped.

After that, and with more preparation for what might happen next, I often attempted to communicate with it, and often it would reply. I quickly discovered that it possessed a rudimentary intelligence similar to that of a dog or cat. It would respond to my initial inquiry and show me that it knew I was trying to contact it, but it did not answer questions or engage in any more complex communication. It was mischievous and moody like a cat, and, perhaps most important of all, its behavior showed a distinct connection to the ebb and flow of my own emotions. If I was in a bad mood, it was in a bad mood.

A few times during its strange life it was even downright malevolent. On one occasion, in front of friends, a large naillike needle flew out of nowhere and into my leg. On other occasions, in the presence of friends, it inflicted tiny bloody gouges in my flesh. At first I felt a stinging sensation, and then, as I watched, a small hole simply appeared in my skin. Needless to say, when these infrequent but hostile manifestations occurred I was often a little frightened, but I slowly came to realize that the poltergeist's malevolence always corresponded to times when I myself was in an unusually negative state of mind. Conversely, its more playful and impish behavior—laying a handful of dried noodles on my chest while I slept or draping all of my clean socks on various houseplants in the house—occurred when I was in my usual brighter moods. It is also important to note that the acts of hostility, like my darker moods, were few and far between, and hence did not overly color the predominately benevolent nature of the poltergeist.

Of equal significance, the poltergeist seemed connected to me in other ways. When I was a child, its activity was more prevalent in my bedroom than in other rooms of the house, and when its behavior seemed directed against anyone, as in the throwing of objects, it was usually directed against me. Of even more significance, when I grew up and left home it left with me, manifesting itself in every house and apartment that I lived in until I was in my mid-twenties. And then, for all practical purposes, it vanished.

The fact that poltergeists seem to center around certain individuals as opposed to "haunting" places has been noted often in the literature that has developed on the phenomenon. A possible biological and/or psychological connection has also been noted, especially in light of the fact that poltergeist phenomena frequently center around children and tend to dwindle away after puberty—although cases such as my own, in which the phenomena continued well into adulthood, are not unheard of. These apparent trends suggest that the poltergeist is not a spirit or ghost at all but is actually an unconscious expression of the latent psychic abilities of its human focus, and this is the explanation I favor. As for how the poltergeist manages to behave almost as if it has a mind of its own, I believe that this is due to the same mechanisms that allow entities in our dreams and even the subpersonalities of individuals with multiple personalities to display a certain amount of autonomy from their psychological parents. In short, I believe that the apparent separateness of the poltergeist from the individual has to do with the "self-organizing" properties of psychological phenomena in general, and more will be said about this in later chapters.

In any case, for some curious and remarkable reason my parents pretty much took our own poltergeist in stride, and this resulted in us coming to view it, in a certain sense, as a family pet. Strange as it may sound to those who have not experienced such things, it became for us as mundane a part of our existence as the sidewalk and the trees, and it wasn't until I was older that I began to realize what an extraordinary thing it really was.

As my curiosity grew I quickly discovered that our poltergeist possessed many striking similarities with other poltergeists reported throughout history. For example, although we had no idea of this fact at the time, poltergeist hauntings often start with showers of gravel on the roof. Indeed, there are accounts of this particular manifestation dating back at least to A.D. 858, when priests were called in to exorcise a supposed demon raining gravel down on, and causing mysterious rappings in, a house near Bingen on the Rhine. Similarly, in the sixteenth century it is recorded in church literature that St. Caesarius of Arles was called in to exorcise the supposed demon responsible for showers of gravel raining down on the house of a deacon named Helpidius, and so on.

I was intrigued to discover that the inexplicable crashing sounds, the teleportation of objects, the strange stigmata, and even the sense of rudimentary intelligence conveyed in the disembodied rappings are all phenomena often mentioned in the available literature on poltergeists. In a recent conversation with physicist Fred Alan Wolf, I asked him if he felt there might be any validity to the poltergeist phenomenon. He replied, "Quantum physics itself asserts that there is some very ghostlike behavior taking place in phenomena in nature. Because physicists are as rooted in the same modality of common sense as everyone else, it's just as ghostlike and weird to us as a so-called ghost would be to someone else. So, therefore, why not poltergeists?" In spite of Dr. Wolf's openness, even as he talked I knew that there were many physicists who would view poltergeist phenomena with less liberal minds.

Perhaps because the poltergeist had been such a prosaic part of my existence, it wasn't until I was an adult that I realized what a dichotomy I represented. I knew that poltergeist phenomena existed, and I was keenly interested in their history and phenomenology. Throughout my youth I had also had a voracious interest in science, and as a child of the technological age I grew up believing, and still believe, that science is one of the most powerful tools for growth that the human race possesses. And yet I still remember the day when the revelation finally hit me that I believed in, and had experienced firsthand, a range of phenomena that science not only is currently incapable of explaining but doesn't even yet acknowledge exists. Certainly I knew that my experience was not commonplace, and the epiphany I underwent was one not of kind but of degree. But somehow, because the poltergeist had been such a matter-of-fact part of my life, I did not realize what a singular experience it was.

It was on that day that I decided to find out more about the poltergeist, not just its history but its deeper workings. It was this search which led me ultimately to the breathtaking new understandings of reality being offered to us by quantum physics. It is my belief that quantum theory, as well as recent discoveries from a number of other different branches of science, holds at least part of the answer to the mystery of the poltergeist.

Science is beginning to tell us about things once considered unknowable. More than that, implicit in the tentative answers that we will explore in this book is a larger message, namely that there are energies not yet glimpsed by science and forces still unknown. Between the lines of what we know about the subatomic landscape, there remain indications of still further regions to be explored, and perhaps entire worlds beyond the quantum.

# 1

# Quantum Physics Comes of Age

> In short, quantum mechanics, special relativity, and realism cannot all be true.
>
> — ARTHUR L. ROBINSON in *Science*

BEFORE we embark on our quest to find out what science has to say about some of the deeper questions of existence, an obvious but important point must be made. Asking a question always presupposes at least some idea of the range of possible answers. For example, at the end of the last century, physicists started asking the question, "What are the basic building blocks of matter?" Implicit in this question was the belief that matter was composed of something that resembled our idea of building blocks. As we will see, one of the most important lessons of quantum physics is that this is simply not the case.

There is another important lesson to be learned from this discovery, and indeed in virtually all of the discoveries of quantum physics. That is, that sometimes the answers to the questions we ask involve concepts that we do not have the capability to visualize directly. This is the the point driven home by the Aspect experiment, which is what this chapter is about. However, before we delve into that historic event in greater detail I would first like to give a few examples.

## PARTICLE SPIN

One of the simplest demonstrations of the fact that the behavior of subatomic particles involves concepts that we are not able to visualize directly can be found in the phenomenon called particle spin.

Those of us who do not know better have a tendency to think of subatomic particles as little planets orbiting in space. This analogy is partially correct, for subatomic particles do possess some of the qualities of the planets, or spheres. For example, physicists find it valid to say that particles rotate about an axis just as Earth rotates on its axis while it revolves around the Sun. However, when compared with one another it has been found that different particles spin in peculiarly different manners, and these differences can be represented by numbers. If the spin of a photon is given a value of 1, an electron has a comparative spin of 1/2. A neutron also has a spin of 1/2, and a particle known as a pion has a spin of 0.

Although the strangeness of this state of affairs may initially elude the layman, in his book *Superforce* Paul Davies provides a way of visualizing what is meant by these numbers. As every schoolchild knows, if you have a globe of Earth and you want to turn it around until it is once again in the same position as it started, you have to turn it a mere 360°. Not so with the electron. If you turn an electron 360° you will find that it is only halfway around. This seems to go against our commonsense understanding of objects and reality, but because the electron has a spin of 1/2, to make it turn one full circle you must turn it yet another 360° (see Figure 1). In other words, unlike spheres as we know them, an electron must be passed through a full 720° in order to make one complete revolution.

Why is this so? Davies suggests that perhaps on the subatomic level reality possesses an extra dimension that requires a full 720° rotation to take in its entire sweep.

360°                                                720°

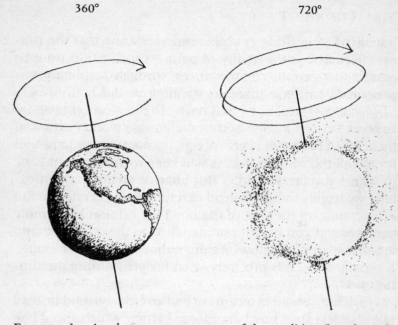

FIGURE 1    *An electron possesses some of the qualities of a sphere, for it is meaningful to speak of it as possessing spin. However, unlike spheres that we are familiar with such as the globe of the planet Earth, an electron must be rotated 720° to make one complete rotation.*

They suggest that effects of this extra dimension come into play only on the level of the very small, and thus, unlike the electron, human beings and other large objects have lost the facility to distinguish one 360° rotation from the next.[1]

Whatever the explanation, the curious extra-dimensionality of the electron does have some measurable effects on our own level of existence. For example, the magnetic field produced by an electron when it spins is exactly twice the value that we might expect it to be if it were produced by the spinning of an electrically charged sphere.[2]

Anomalous spins are only one of the strange properties of particles in the subatomic landscape.

## THE TUNNEL EFFECT

Equally disconcerting is a phenomenon known as the tunnel effect. This is the ability of particles such as electrons to pass, under certain circumstances, through seemingly impenetrable barriers. Imagine standing at the bottom of a huge stainless steel bowl and trying to roll a cannon ball up the bowl's steep incline and to the outside world beyond. If the edge of the bowl is very steep, no matter how hard you try to roll the cannon ball, it will keep returning right back to where you are standing. But imagine giving it a particularly vigorous toss and instead of returning, at a certain point in its transit up the side of the bowl the cannon ball simply vanishes and you hear it rematerialize on the other side and fall to the ground below. Again, although this goes against common sense, it is precisely what happens during the tunnel effect.

Imagine instead of a cannon ball an electron, and instead of a stainless steel bowl an energy barrier, which should be an effective obstacle to an electron. If the energy barrier is strong enough, an electron fired at it will simply bounce back. But unlike a cannon ball, an electron seems to know beforehand the limitations of the obstacle it is approaching. If the energy barrier is a little weaker, instead of bouncing back, the electron will disappear before reaching the barrier and rematerialize on the other side. As Rockefeller University physicist Heinz Pagels says, "right through the wall."[3]

The tunnel effect also has measurable effects on the level of everyday life. For example, it has been discovered that tunneling can be used to amplify electronic signals. In practical application this has enabled us to develop such technological advances as transistors. To some extent quantum tunneling is also responsible for nuclear radioactivity. Like the stainless steel bowl in the cannon ball experiment, the nucleus itself acts like a wall that imprisons the particles it will eventually emit as radioactivity.[4]

## PARTICLES HAVE NO PRECISE LOCATION

If particle spin and the tunneling effect have not dispelled the notion that subatomic particles are not objects as we know them, pointing out one final characteristic they possess will. Subatomic particles also have a wavelike nature, and this, among other things, means that it is sometimes very difficult to speak of them as even existing in any single and precise location.

This disturbing fact was first clearly articulated in the early part of this century by the German physicist Werner Heisenberg, one of quantum theory's founding fathers, in his now famous uncertainty principle. What Heisenberg's uncertainty principle dealt with specifically is the idea of trajectory. For example, when a bullet is fired from a gun, both classical physics and our commonsense notions of the world tell us that it is possible at any given moment to measure both the bullet's speed and its position in order to chart its path as it hurtles through space. This path is the bullet's trajectory.

What Heisenberg pointed out is that it is impossible to do the same for a subatomic particle such as an electron. Using one experimental method, we may determine its speed or momentum. Using another experimental method, we may determine its position. But we can never perform both measurements simultaneously. Consequently, we may know that at one instant an electron is leaving a source, and we may know that a few moments later it is striking a photographic plate. But we can never know how it got from its source to the plate. As Heisenberg's uncertainty principle articulates, it is thus completely meaningless to speak of a particle as possessing a trajectory, or path of continuously connected points through space. University of Texas physicist John Wheeler has likened the particle to a Great Smoky Dragon whose head and tail we can locate, but whose body is destined to remain forever lost in an indecipherable mist.

It is important to note that the fact that we can never know a particle's place and motion at the same time is not merely the result of some clumsiness in our ability to measure it. It is a quality intrinsic to the subatomic world, and once again its effects can be perceived on our own level of existence. For example, one of the most basic tenets of physics is that when you cool a substance it passes through progressively denser states; water freezes into ice, and so on. Even gases can be frozen, as anyone who has handled dry ice or frozen carbon dioxide can attest. However, physicists have discovered that helium never becomes a solid, no matter how cold it gets. This is because helium atoms are so much lighter than the atoms of other elements, and the repulsive forces of its electrons are configured in such a way that to pack them close enough to form a solid would violate the quantum uncertainty of their position. This is something that nature does not allow.[5]

The fact that a particle seems to possess a certain degree of uncertainty about where it is is only part of the problem. It even seems to be unsure about what it is, on some occasions displaying the characteristics of a particle and on other occasions displaying the characteristics of a wave. To explain how the quantum physicist accounts for this seeming paradox brings us to the very crux of quantum theory, and a three-hundred-year-old debate that began with Sir Isaac Newton and culminated only recently with the Aspect experiment.

## BODIES INTO LIGHT

3 In 1690, the great Dutch physicist Christian Huygens advanced his theory that light was transmitted in spherical waves spreading out from the luminous source. Because waves, like the waves in an ocean, cannot exist without a supporting medium, Huygens further postulated that such waves of light were transmitted through space on a ghostly

and hypothetical substance he called ether. He based his theory on the fact that light possesses the ability to diffract. That is, it is slightly deflected from a straight line when it passes over the edge of an opaque object. For example, rays of light passing through a small opening into a dark room spread more widely on the opposite wall than straight lines from source to wall would warrant. Huygens confessed, however, that he was unable to explain why, when it was not being diffracted, light was able to travel in such unerringly straight lines.

For idiosyncratic reasons Sir Isaac Newton was more persuaded by light's ability to travel in straight lines. He rejected Huygens' wave theory of light and in 1704 published his own belief that because light did travel in straight lines when it was not being diffracted, it must therefore be composed of innumerable tiny particles, or corpuscles, moving through space. Needing no ether in his theory to explain how such particles were transmitted, he rejected that also. Like Huygens, however, he confessed that he was unable to explain the phenomenon of diffraction.

At the end of his treatise on light, Newton also listed thirty-one queries for further consideration. Among these strangely prophetic questions was one that seemed as intuitively brilliant as it was poetic. "Why may not Nature change light into bodies," Newton asked, "and bodies into light?"

Had Sir Isaac and his illustrious rival realized that the paradox that light behaves on some occasions as a wave and on other occasions as a particle was not an indication that one of their theories was in error, but an anomaly intrinsic to the fabric of reality itself, they might have invented quantum theory on the spot.

About a century later another physicist tilted the scales, for a time, in favor of Huygens. In 1801, an English physicist named Thomas Young proved beyond the shadow of a doubt that light possessed certain properties that could only be associated with a wave. Young, a medical doctor before he became a physicist, was also the first to give descriptions of astigmatism, blood pressure, and capillary attraction. To understand what Young did it is first necessary to understand a little about a phenomenon that physicists call interference.

In everyday usage, interference obviously refers to a situation in which one thing interferes with another. In physics it means pretty much the same, except that it refers to very specific situations in which one wavelike phenomenon or stream of vibration interferes with another. For example, imagine that you are standing on a bridge that crosses over a still pond. In each hand you hold a pebble, and you simultaneously drop the pebbles about a foot apart into the water below. As each pebble hits the water it causes a series of concentric rings to ripple outward from the point of impact and, where the rings from each impact cross, they either undulate with the rings from the other impact or disrupt them. In either case, the crisscross pattern where the rings intersect is interference.

When two phenomena are able to interfere with each other in this manner, a physicist can tell that they are spread out over space and are, therefore, wavelike. Conversely, phenomena that are not spread out over space, like particles, would not be expected to interfere with each other anymore than the two falling pebbles might be expected to suddenly reach out and interfere with each other as they plummet toward the water's surface.

What Young did in his now famous experiment is to perform a variation on Huygens' demonstration that light possesses the ability to diffract. To do this he allowed a small light source to shine through two narrow slits cut in a piece of opaque material. After the light passed through the slits he then allowed it to project onto a screen. What he discovered was that instead of ending up with just two bands of light on the second screen as would be expected if light were composed of particles passing like little bullets through the two adjacent slits, he ended up with a series of bright and dark bands of varying intensity (see Figure 2). Young concluded that such a phenomenon or pattern of interference could only be explained if one assumed that light possessed wavelike properties.

FIGURE 2  *The double-slit experiment. The fact that a beam of light passed through two slits creates more than two bands of light on a screen reveals light's wavelike properties.*

After much debate it was generally accepted that light was a wave, and this view persisted for about another hundred years. Then two events occurred that brought back the old debate with a vengeance. The first was a discovery that is not generally considered to be the founding of quantum theory. In 1900, while studying the way that objects glow when they are heated to very high temperatures, the German physicist Max Planck discovered that the frequency of the radiation given off by the objects as they grew hotter did not rise continuously but in clearly defined spurts. In the classical understanding of physics this was as strange as if one had happened upon a stream where the water did not flow continuously, but moved along in great glacierlike chunks followed by moving patches of dryness. As Planck later put it, out of "sheer desperation" he proposed that the radiation emitted by such objects must therefore be "quantized" or divided into spurts of energy he called quanta.

The second event came five years later when young Albert Einstein made a stupendous conceptual leap, proposing that even energy itself is quantized. In studying the photoelectric effect—the ability of a beam of light to cause a metal surface to give off electrons—Einstein became convinced that the metal was reacting as if it was being struck not by waves but by little particles. As a result he once again advanced the outrageous notion that light really should be viewed as composed of particles, or discrete quanta he called "photons." The two-hundred-year-old debate had come full circle.

For a time Einstein's assertion was widely greeted with skepticism and even derision. After all, Young's demonstration that light possessed wavelike properties seemed indisputable. It wasn't until 1923 that Einstein's photon theory of light received experimental vindication. That same year a young French physicist named Louis de Broglie dropped another bombshell. Intrigued by the notion that light, which so clearly behaved as if it was a wave, could sometimes behave as if it was a particle, de Broglie wondered if particles like the electron might also sometimes behave as if they were waves. Using the equations of Planck and Einstein, de Broglie sketched out a mathematical picture of the possible wavelength of such a particle, and two years later his predictions were experimentally confirmed. It seemed that not only were waves particles, but particles were also waves. In some strange way Newton's prophecy (which was also to be proved correct in another way with Einstein's $E = mc^2$ equation) had come true. Light had been turned into bodies and bodies into light.

What did it all mean? At first the world of physics was in an uproar. The evidence was as clear as it was perplexing. The universe was composed of quanta that could behave at times as if they were particles and at other times as if they were waves. The only problem was that such a state of existence does not manifest itself on the level of everyday life. For example, when one is in a boat on choppy waters, one does not see the water hovering between two states of existence, composed, first, of waves, which fade suddenly into a shower of bullets and then turn back again into waves.

In his classic remark, Heisenberg summed up his own confusion on the matter as follows:

I remember discussions with Bohr which went through many hours till very late at night and ended almost in despair; and when at the end of the discussion I went alone for a walk in the neighboring park I repeated to myself again and again the question: Can nature possibly be as absurd as it seemed to us in these atomic experiments?[6]

To resolve the seeming paradox of the wave/particle duality of the universe some physicists suggested that perhaps matter should not be thought of as composed of particles, but as matter waves. Others pointed out that this wasn't acceptable because devices could be constructed that could record the passage of subatomic particles, and the tracks they left were straight lines, not rippling wave fronts. In the end, one of the most persuasive schools of thought resolved that the wavelike aspect of particles was not waves of *matter*, but should more accurately be thought of as waves of *probability*. This became one of the more acceptable interpretations of quantum physics, but it also brought with it disturbing implications for our understanding of reality.

For example, in Young's double-slit experiment the bands of interference produced by photons as they pass through the two slits very clearly reveal light's wavelike nature. However, if the opaque screen on which the beams are projected is replaced by a piece of photographic film, each photon that strikes the plate will leave only one point of impact in the photographic emulsion. This very clearly reveals the photon's particlelike nature. The disturbing implications for our understanding of reality come into play when the photons are allowed to hurtle toward the double-slit one at a time.

When this happens each photon that passes through the double-slit filter once again strikes the photographic film and leaves a single imprint of its collision. However, as more and more photons are allowed to pass through the double-slit filter and one by one leave their mark in the photographic emulsion, the pattern of interference still arises (see Figure 3). If one of the slits is covered, the pattern no longer emerges. The question is, How does any given photon know when the second slit is open and when it is not? If each photon is only passing through one slit, how does it know the status of the other slit and, hence, what sort of pattern to build up on the photograph?

The answer given by quantum physics is as astonishing as it is profound. It is that each photon somehow goes through both openings *at the same time* and thus carries some sort of knowledge of the status of both slits when it strikes the photograph. In other words, while the photon is still in the Great Smoky Dragon phase of its transit, *it does not exist as a single object.* During this phase it quite literally seems able to manifest as several probabilistic counterparts of itself and explores all possible pathways open to it simultaneously. It is only when it reaches the photographic plate and leaves a single point of impact that it appears to abandon its multiple existences and once again returns to behaving like a solitary projectile. It should be noted that although this experiment involved photons, electrons and many other subatomic particles have also been found to possess the ability to exist in several different probable states simultaneously. This is why

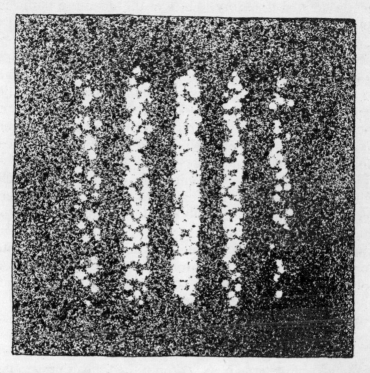

FIGURE 3   *Even if a beam of light is passed through the double-slit one photon at a time, the photons will still build up in several bands in a speckled sort of way, revealing that they are behaving both as if they are particles and as if they are waves.*

physicists speak of the wavelike phases of such particles not as material waves, but as waves of probability.

Needless to say, the ability of subatomic particles to exist in more than one place at the same time raises a number of very profound questions. One involves a controversy that has surfaced repeatedly in the history of quantum physics. That is, what is the role of the human observer in all of this? For example, just as Heisenberg's uncertainty principle makes it meaningless to speak of a particle as possessing a clearly defined trajectory in space, the quantum particle's ability to be in more than one place at the same time before it collides with a measuring device also seems to make it meaningless to speak of it as possessing any definite reality in the absence of a human (or other) observer.

For example, before the single photon in the double-slit experiment has made its mark on the photographic plate, the most that we can say about it is that it is ghostlike and seems to exist along all of its possible pathways at once. However, even after it strikes the photographic plate, no amount of scientific ingenuity can determine precisely where it struck until we actually look at the plate and see. We can determine the probability of it striking this place or that, but the photon does not step up out of the fog of its multiple existences and reveal a single point of impact until an observer enters the picture. This seems to suggest that consciousness is more deeply connected to the ultimate stuff of the universe than was previously suspected in science, but this is a very controversial point and one that we will discuss more fully in later chapters.

A second important question is, If the subatomic building blocks of material objects do not themselves possess the characteristics of material objects, how real is the material world that we inhabit? In other words, at what level and by what strange magic does nature allow the apparent solidity of the world to disintegrate into the phantomlike and schizophrenic multiplicity of probabilities that is the subatomic realm?

In the early days of quantum physics some physicists refused to accept that such a disintegration occurred at all. The most distinguished proponent of this point of view was Einstein himself. In spite of the fact that he had assisted in the creation of quantum theory, he was deeply disturbed by the picture of subatomic reality it proposed. He remained convinced that behind the ghostlike and baffling world it described lay a more comforting and classical level of reality in which objects would once again be found to possess such precise and clearly defined properties as location and trajectory. As he wrote in a letter to his lifelong friend, the distinguished German physicist, Max Born, "Even the great initial success of the quantum theory does not make me believe . . . although I am well aware that our younger colleagues interpret this as a consequence of senility. No doubt the day will come when we will see whose instinctive attitude was the correct one."[7]

To bring this day nearer, Einstein was forever playing devil's advocate, and continually poked away at the theoretical structure of quantum theory in hopes of finding some place where it might crumble. It was while searching for one of these flaws of reasoning that he formulated a puzzle that eventually led Aspect and his group to perform their historic experiment. However, as we will see, in mounting his attack Einstein made a fatal error. He assumed without question that objective reality exists.

## THE ASPECT EXPERIMENT

On the receiving end of many of Einstein's attacks was the great Danish physicist, Neils Bohr. Whereas Werner Heisenberg was one of the chief architects of the mathematical formalism behind quantum theory, Bohr's forte was to interpret the difficult conceptual implications of that formalism. As a result, whenever Bohr and Einstein met they would argue the points on which they differed.

In one of their most famous confrontations, at a physics conference in 1930, Einstein asserted that he had found a flaw in Heisenberg's uncertainty principle. More precisely, the object of his attack was the principle's assertion that just as it is impossible to know simultaneously both position and momentum of a quantum, it is also impossible to know both its energy and the precise moment at which it possesses that energy. In formulating his offensive, Einstein employed his own famous $E = mc^2$ equation. According to this equation energy, $E$, like matter itself, possesses mass. Thus, one way of measuring energy is quite literally to weigh it.

With this understanding, Einstein formulated his argument as follows. Consider a box with a hole in one of its walls that can be opened or closed with a shutter controlled by a clock inside the box. The clock and shutter mechanisms are designed to open the hole for a very brief interval, long enough to allow only one photon, generated by a built-in light source, to escape from the box. The clock is also designed to record the precise time that it releases the photon.

So far such a setup would present no problem to Heisenberg's uncertainty principle. Where the problem seems to come in is when Einstein suggested that the entire box, clock and all, be weighed both before and after the experiment. In this way, Einstein pointed out, one could measure both the instant the photon was released and the change in the box's mass, thus deducing the photon's energy.

One witness at the conference wrote, "It was quite a shock for Bohr. . . . During the whole evening he was extremely unhappy, going from one to the other and trying to persuade them that it couldn't be true, that it would be the end of physics if Einstein were right; but he couldn't produce any refutation."[8] Einstein and Bohr left the conference together, Einstein wearing an ironical smile and Bohr still deeply flustered. It wasn't until the next morning, and after many long hours of thought, that Bohr came back with the solution.

As he pointed out, it seemed that Einstein had himself sown the seeds of his own defeat. According to Einstein's own theory of relativity, time is affected by gravity. Since the box cannot be weighed unless gravity is present, gravity's effect on time must also be figured into the equations. When this is done, Bohr revealed that quantum uncertainty returns exactly as predicted.

Einstein continued to stew, and in 1935 he advanced the

most famous of his attacks against quantum theory in a
paper coauthored by Boris Podolsky and Nathan Rosen. The
goal of the Einstein-Podolsky-Rosen paper was once again
to challenge quantum theory's allegation that quantum uncertainty was absolute.

To accomplish such a feat, Einstein, Podolsky, and Rosen
proposed another thought experiment. Given that one
couldn't simultaneously measure certain sets of properties
in a single particle, they proposed that perhaps one could
measure both quantities with the assistance of a second particle, one whose properties are connected in some way to
the first. The example that follows is similar to the subatomic
process they used to illustrate their point but is easier to
visualize.

Consider a highly volatile little atom physicists call positronium. The positronium atom consists of a single electron
combined with a positron (the electron's antiparticle). Because of the positronium's instability, the electron and the
positron often annihilate each other, and the atom decays
into two photons traveling in opposite directions. The significant feature of this decay is that when they are measured,
the two photons are always found to possess identical angles
of polarization (polarization is the spatial orientation of a
light wave as it travels away from its source).

Using the example of the photons, what Einstein and his
colleagues suggested, in essence, was that if quantum uncertainty did not allow one to determine the polarization of
one photon, one could determine it by measuring the polarization of the other photon. Theoretically, one could simultaneously obtain two pieces of information about a single
photon, and Heisenberg's uncertainty principle would once
again be violated.

Bohr's counter for this line of reasoning was well
known. The error that Einstein, Podolsky, and Rosen were
making in structuring their argument, Bohr said, is that they
were assuming that subatomic systems existed objectively,

and that it was meaningful to speak of the polarization of any given photon as existing before a measurement has been made. This, in Bohr's view, was simply not the case. Bohr maintained that on the quantum level reality is *intrinsically* blurry and a precise angle of polarization for any given photon does not yet exist until a human observer has entered the picture and lifted it up out of the probabilistic blur of the quantum landscape. Quantum uncertainty is preserved because there is no way of knowing how performing a measurement on one photon has disturbed the system as a whole. Performing a different measurement on the second photon may give you two pieces of information, but you have no right to say that the two pieces of information ever simultaneously applied to a single photon.

Einstein, Podolsky, and Rosen anticipated this argument and incorporated their response into their paper. If Bohr was right, if subatomic reality was an irreducible fog of probabilities and it was meaningless to speak of a specific angle of polarization as existing before a measurement had been made, then another problem developed. Imagine, for example, that you have allowed a positronium atom to decay and instead of performing a measurement right away, you allow one of its photons to travel to one side of the galaxy and the other photon to travel to the other side of the galaxy. You have arranged for laboratories to be set up on both ends of the galaxy, and when one of the photons reaches its receiving station, a measurement is performed to determine its polarization. If the angle of a photon's polarization does not yet exist until a measurement is made, and the second photon is found to have an identical angle of polarization (as our experience with positronium atoms tells us it will), then that means that somehow the first photon has instantaneously communicated its angle to its twin across the galaxy.

This, said Einstein, Podolsky, and Rosen, was an entirely unacceptable state of affairs. Measurements on one particle should no more affect its twin on the opposite side of the galaxy than striking a cue ball in London should cause a ball in Calcutta to instantaneously go into the side pocket. As Einstein pointed out, if such an event were found to be taking place it would imply the existence of some sort of "ghostly action-at-a-distance." And as Einstein, Podolsky, and Rosen stated in their paper, "No reasonable definition of reality could be expected to permit this."[9]

One of the reasons for the strength of Einstein's conviction on this matter was a discovery he had made while formulating his special theory of relativity. Einstein discovered that time is not absolute in the universe, but is relative to the velocity of the observer. For example, it can be demonstrated mathematically that a clock traveling *near* the velocity of light will move slower than one that is stationary. A clock traveling *at* the speed of light would stop completely. Einstein deduced that nothing could ever travel faster than light, because for such an object the time barrier would cease to exist. Instantaneous communication was impossible, since signals might actually be sent into the future and the past, implying all sorts of unacceptable paradoxes in nature. Hence, Einstein concluded that quantum theory was incompatible with any reasonable idea of reality, and therefore incomplete.

The publication of Einstein, Podolsky, and Rosen's paper created quite a stir among physicists, but because it was just a thought experiment, there was no immediately apparent way the matter could actually be put to the test. The debate between Bohr and Einstein remained unresolved.

It wasn't until 1964 that John Bell, a physicist at the European Organization for Nuclear Research (CERN) in Switzerland, thought of a way in which an actual experiment might be set up to settle the matter once and for all. In a brilliant mathematical proof now known as Bell's theorem, Bell showed that if quantum theory was correct, one had to accept at least one of two options—either the world was nonobjective and did not exist in a definite state, or it was "nonlocal," with instantaneous action-at-a-distance. It was as simple as that.

What Bell did was to design an experimental method by which the level of correlation between photons could be measured. As he demonstrated, if reality was objective, as Einstein had assumed, then a certain maximum level of correlation would be found when the experiment was performed. However, if reality was not objective, or if some sort of instantaneous action-at-a-distance was taking place, a higher level of correlation would be found. In either case, the great debate between Bohr and Einstein could at last be put to the test.

The only remaining problem was that the experiment outlined by Bell required a level of technological precision that was not available in the 1960s. In 1972, physicists John F. Clauser and Stuart Freedman of Lawrence Livermore Laboratory devised an experiment which suggested that some sort of action-at-a-distance was taking place, but their methodology was criticized for various reasons.

Then, in 1982, Alain Aspect, along with colleagues Jean Dalibard and Gérard Roger, added the refinements necessary to make the results unequivocal. The group used photons produced by atoms of mercury vapor excited into a higher energy state with a laser beam as their paired particles. Then, with the aid of switching mechanisms that could operate in the billionths of a second, fast enough to catch a photon after it had left its source but before it had traveled more than a few yards away, Aspect, Dalibard, and Roger proceeded to measure the angles of polarization of a stream of countless paired photons. When they finished they added up the level of correlations between them and discovered that it was far greater than would be expected if subatomic particles obeyed the same rules as objects as we know them.[10] Einstein had been wrong, and Bohr had been right. Quantum physics had come of age.

But what does it all mean? In an apparent manifestation of the Limit Syndrome, some physicists still side with Einstein and staunchly oppose the notion that Aspect's findings suggest the possibility of faster-than-light communication. The reason they give for their position is that although the polarizations of any two photons are found to be instantaneously correlated no matter how far apart they are when the measurements are taken, the values obtained for any given measurement are completely random. Thus, there is no way to control the correlation and employ it to send a signal.

To visualize why this is so, imagine that you have two people in different parts of the world, one in an apartment in Paris and the other in an apartment in New York. Each person is sitting at a table with a completely shuffled deck of playing cards in front of him. However, these are not just ordinary decks of cards. They were sold to you by a wizard who told you that they had a powerful magic spell on them that turned them into "quantum playing cards." As the wizard explained, this means that cards drawn from both decks simultaneously will always be identical.

Being skeptical, you have given the cards to friends in both Paris and New York to test them, and as the test proceeds you discover that, just as the wizard promised, each time the person in Paris draws a card from the deck, the person in New York also draws the same card. Over and over you discover this to be true (see Figure 4). Even when the cards are drawn at precisely the same moment—leaving no time for them to communicate with each other—they are always identical. Furthermore, you discover that the cards remain magically connected no matter how far apart you move the decks. At first it seems that you have discovered a way to communicate instantaneously across limitless distances. The only problem is that the wizard has warned you that the magic of the cards only works when the cards are completely shuffled and facedown. Thus, although the

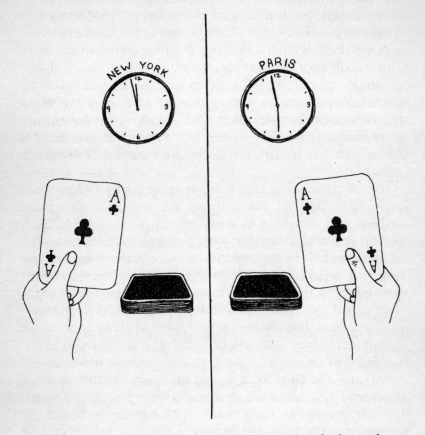

FIGURE 4   *A quantum deck of cards. Even though the cards are thoroughly shuffled and there is no way to determine which card will come up next, a card drawn in New York will always be identical to a card drawn from its sister deck in Paris.*

cards are always instantaneously connected, you have no way to control which card comes up next. The sequences are always completely random. As a result you cannot arrange the cards into even the simplest of a dot-dash sequences without destroying their magic. To your dismay you find that the marvelous telephone line you have stumbled upon does stretch through space and time in seemingly miraculous ways, but it is clogged with an impenetrable static.

The existence of such static notwithstanding, other physicists still believe that the fact that such correlations can occur at all implies that we should take faster-than-light signaling more seriously. As Brian Josephson, who won a Nobel Prize in 1973 for his work on quantum tunneling and superconductivity, stated in a 1982 interview, "It raises the possibility that one part of the universe may have knowledge of another part—some kind of contact at a distance under certain conditions."[11]

At the aforementioned 1986 conference on quantum measurement held in New York, other physicists argued similar points of view. They believed that the instantaneous correlations between paired particles may indeed have practical and usable applications. To further their argument, a number of scientists are currently in the process of devising experiments they hope will prove that quantum mechanical effects are not confined to the subatomic world, but may also be reproducible on the level of everyday life.

At the conference Jean-Pierre Vigier of the Institut Henri Poincaré in Paris outlined an experiment he believes will show that information is actually being propagated between particles at 7.57 times the speed of light. To do this Vigier plans to construct a device that will determine whether a single neutron will interfere with itself in a specially designed double-slit apparatus. Then, by blocking both possible paths of the neutron with a device sensitive to the neutron's spin, Vigier hopes to learn more about how the neutron manages to be in two places at once.[12]

Following a different tack, Sean Washburn and Richard A. Webb of the IBM Watson Research Center offer evidence that they have already designed an experiment that shows that quantum tunneling effects are not limited to the microscopic world. By employing a device known as a SQUID, a Superconducting Quantum Interference Device, they assert that they have found evidence that macroscopic quantum tunneling effects can also occur.[13]

Similarly, Claudia Tesche of the IBM Watson Research Center also believes that quantum mechanical magic can spill over into everyday reality. By placing electrons in the bottom of energy wells—much like the stainless steel bowls in the previously mentioned description of quantum tunneling—and then sloshing the wells back and forth, she also hopes to demonstrate that the strange schizophrenia of subatomic particles can have macroscopic effects.[14] In a recent article on her work, science writer D. E. Thomsen says that if Tesche's experiment is a success, "we could then find ourselves in the situation where the left hand can know what the right is doing in ways that it couldn't under classical physics. . . ."[15]

As for the physicists who remain skeptical of such possibilities, at least some researchers accuse them of not facing up to the profound implication of Aspect's findings. Says Dr. Fritz Rohrlich of Syracuse University, such physicists have developed their own sort of schizophrenia when it comes to interpreting the Aspect results: "On one hand they accept the standard interpretation of quantum theory, including the epistemological irreducibility of system and observer. On the other they insist on the reality of quantum systems even when these are not observed."[16]

At this point, it is perhaps important to make a comment about language. Because this is such a controversial issue, many physicists become highly meticulous in their choice of words to describe what is going on in the Aspect experiment. For example, many would still bristle if one were to say that the two photons are "connected" and would prefer to say only that measurements performed on them are "correlated." A more important distinction comes in when referring to what might be responsible for these connections and or correlations. As we have seen, one explanation is that they are indeed brought about by a "faster-than-light" signaling process, but some physicists eschew this choice of words. Of these, some prefer to say that they are due to "nonlocal causes." That is, whatever the connection or correlation is between them, it does not move faster than the speed of light. It simply moves through a part of the universe that is nonlocal, perhaps through some dimensional doorway. But even this is a point of view that many physicists avoid.

This is a difficult but very important issue. On one hand, such distinctions of language are a necessary evil because the quantum world does not always lend itself to the terminology we use in everyday life. This was a point stressed by Bohr even into his final years—that to avoid being encumbered by preconceived and possible incorrect ideas about reality we must be very careful with the words we choose to describe quantum events. But on the other hand, such an approach to language can become so esoteric that it may cloud and obscure important issues.

For example, some physicists shy away from both the ideas of nonlocal causes and faster-than-light signaling. They say only that measurements on the two photons are "correlated" and leave it at that. By labeling the phenomenon with a new terminology, they feel that they have explained all there is to explain about what is going on between the two photons.

Others reject this point of view. In his 1984 book, *In Search of Reality*, Barnard d'Espagnat, a leading authority on the conceptual foundations of quantum theory and the author of numerous works on the subject, argues that the Aspect experiment has indeed posed questions which now must be answered by science. Similarly, Paul Davies agrees that the Aspect experiment has put the last nail in the coffin of commonsense physics. He feels that at the very least Aspect's disarming findings have "some very profound implications for the nature of the physical world."[17]

This is the point of view that I find the most persuasive.

The puzzle uncovered by the Aspect experiment demands more than just a new label to explain it. The correlation of measurements made on quantum particles over vast stretches of space and time is not simply a meaningless glitch in the fabric of the universe, an inconsequential anomaly to be glanced at briefly and then swept under the carpet.

Why do many physicists believe that no further explanation lies beyond the correlation of the two photons? At least some have suggested that the eagerness to seize upon the word "correlation" as a permanent philosophical cul-de-sac is just a "ready excuse to avoid the trouble of further deep thought."[18]

One of the few scientists who refuse to believe that it is a philosophical cul-de-sac and who have attempted to probe deeper and describe the level of reality that may lie beneath these correlations is an eminent theoretical physicist and former protégé of Einstein named David Bohm. Bohm recently published an in-depth account of the worlds he believes exist beyond the quantum, and his astonishing suggestions of what those worlds may be like are the subject of the next chapter.

About the only thing that most physicists agree on is that the Aspect experiment has confirmed that Bohr was right. At the level of the quantum, reality *is* fuzzy, and when we attempt to penetrate that mist, our commonsense understanding of the way the world should work collapses. This, then, is the message of the quantum, and there are two important reasons why we should consider it carefully: First, the implications of quantum theory will profoundly change our understanding of ourselves and our role in the universe. Second, and equally important, is its ability to transform the way we think. As was mentioned at the beginning of this chapter, the answers to the questions we ask sometimes involve concepts that are beyond our current intellectual vocabulary. Thus, many of the disconcerting puzzles of quantum physics should be viewed as transformative mechanisms, new computer programs that we can slip into the biocomputers we call our minds to reprogram and transform them for new ways of thinking. Take a moment, then, to reprogram and ponder the strangeness of the quantum landscape, for as we will see, quantum physics is not the only branch of science that is gently pulling us toward an entirely new way of looking at things.

# 2

# A Higher Multidimensional Reality

> Bohm's challenge to physics is multifarious, detailed, highly mathematical, and revolutionary. Although physicists of his own age are unlikely to want to look into the challenge he poses, as they have now shown such reluctance to do so for more than 30 years, younger scientists have been showing increased interest in his ideas.
>
> — ROBERT TEMPLE in *New Scientist*

IN 1951, a brilliant young Princeton physicist named David Bohm wrote what many consider the classic textbook on Bohr's interpretation of quantum theory. However, shortly after the book's publication, Bohm began to have second thoughts. While he accepted Bohr's conclusion that the world is fuzzy and indeterministic at the quantum level, he no longer viewed the fuzziness of the subatomic landscape as a final truth.

Bohm sent copies of his book to Bohr and Einstein. Bohr did not reply, but Einstein invited him to discuss the quandary of the quantum. In his conversations with Einstein, Bohm's thinking began to depart even more radically from Bohr's. Bohm saw in the Einstein-Podolsky-Rosen experiment something important that quantum theory could not yet explain.[1]

Shortly thereafter Bohm published a paper hypothesizing that "hidden variables" explained the mysterious connections between subatomic particles, such as those between the two photons emitted in the decay of a positronium atom. To this day, many physicists incorrectly perceive that Bohm attempted to impose a determinism on the indeterministic world of the quantum—to dispel the fuzziness Bohr attributed intrinsically to the subatomic landscape. Bohm never intended to restore certainty to the quantum world. On the contrary, as he conceived of them, these hidden variables, if they did exist, existed on a deeper level of reality than manifested itself in quantum uncertainty.[2] As Bohm concedes, his notion did not " 'catch on' among physicists."[3]

As the years passed, Bohm's list of achievements grew. He gained wide respect for his work in plasma physics and authored numerous books and articles, including a distinguished study of the role of chance and causality in physics. He also continued to revise his notion of hidden variables, and while doing so, in the late 1950s, he encountered the work of the Indian philosopher Krishnamurti.[4]

Bohm befriended Krishnamurti in 1961, and their relationship seems to have had an important effect on Bohm's thinking, an impact that, at least in part, aided him in further developing his ideas about hidden variables.[5] This further development ultimately resulted in the 1980 publication of his book *Wholeness and the Implicate Order*, which contains his most recent ideas about what the correlations between subatomic particles suggest about the universe.

Even before Aspect gave quantum theory its final vindication, enough other evidence had accumulated to convince Bohm that subatomic particles were correlated with each other in ways that defied our classical understanding of reality. However, he did not feel that the instantaneous correlations between such particles were due to some sort of faster-than-light signaling process. Instead, Bohm concluded that their existence suggested a nonlocal level of reality beyond the quantum. That is, what we perceive as separate particles in a subatomic system are not really separate at all, but on a deeper level of reality are merely extensions of the same fundamental something. Bohm called the level of reality in which the particles appear to be separate —the level that we inhabit—the *explicate* order. The deeper substratum of reality, the level in which separateness vanishes and all things appear to become part of an unbroken whole, he called the *implicate* order.

To illustrate how a level of unbroken wholeness might explain such correlations without involving faster-than-light signaling processes, Bohm gave the following example. Imagine an aquarium in which a fish swims. Imagine also that there are two television cameras directed at the aquarium. One, which we will call camera *A,* is directed at the front of the aquarium. The other, camera *B,* is directed at the aquarium's side, and each camera is hooked up to a corresponding television monitor. Imagine that you cannot see the aquarium or the fish directly, but only have knowledge of them from the two images you see on the television screens (see Figure 5).

As Bohm pointed out, when you look at the screen, because you only know the fish from the monitors, you might assume that what you are watching is really two fish. However, as you continue to watch, in time you begin to realize that when the fish on monitor *A* moves, the fish on monitor *B* also makes a corresponding movement. If you continue to think of the fish as two separate fish you might incorrectly assume that some sort of instantaneous communication must be occurring between the two fish, but this is not the case. The instantaneous correlations between the movements of the two fish are due instead to the fact that on a deeper level of reality, the reality of the aquarium, the two fish are not really separate entities at all.

According to Bohm's way of thinking, this is roughly analogous to what is going on when we measure the correlations between the two photons in the Einstein-Podolsky-Rosen experiment. In this view the two television monitors

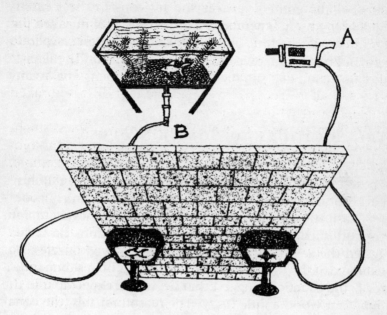

FIGURE 5 *Bohm believed that subatomic particles are ultimately connected in the same way as two different images of the same fish when viewed on two separate television monitors. In both cases the apparent separateness of both such images is an illusion.*

correspond to the world as we know it—the explicate order. The fish as it really exists in the aquarium corresponds to the deeper level of reality that exists beyond the quantum— the implicate order. Put another way, the images on the television screens are really two-dimensional *projections* (or facets) of a three-dimensional reality. Given that two three-dimensional entities such as the photons in the Einstein-Podolsky-Rosen experiment can behave as if they are part of an equally startling and unbroken wholeness, it follows, says Bohm, that our own three-dimensional world is therefore the projection of a still higher and multidimensional reality.

## THE SOLUTIONS TO SOME UNSOLVED PUZZLES

These are not just philosophical speculations on Bohm's part. Bohm, along with his University of London collaborator, Basil Hiley, has worked out the mathematics that might support such a world view, and his equations have suggested the solutions to a number of unsolved puzzles. For example, if the universe really is nonlocal on a subquantum level, the equations suggest that we would expect to find the quantum world a little fuzzy. The reason for this, the equations suggest, is that in a nonlocal universe it would be meaningless to speak about any given arbitrary group of subatomic particles without taking into account their multitudinous linkages with the more than $10^{89}$ other particles in the universe.[6] In other words, as we approach the level of nonlocality it would become increasingly less effective to try to divide such an unbroken wholeness up into what we consider its parts.

According to Bohm and Hiley, only when we begin to deal with relatively large assemblages of particles do such influences cancel out and permit us to speak of systems in isolation. Such large assemblages of particles would include most of the objects we encounter on the level of everyday life, from wristwatches to planetary systems, and that, they suggest, is why classical physics has previously been so successful in describing such phenomena.

In his book, Bohm suggests that the ultimately nonlocal nature of the quantum may explain other puzzles as well.

For example, when a photon seems to go through both slits in the double-slit experiment at once, this confounds our commonsense understanding of the world because we insist upon thinking of the photon as possessing a single location in space and time. However, if Bohm is correct, this is simply not the case. Under certain circumstances the three-dimensional projection of the photon might appear to have a specific location. But because the photon is really a projection of a single and higher-dimensional reality, it is not rigidly confined to the rules of our three-dimensional universe.

Bohm even suggests that the nonlocal nature of the world beyond the quantum might explain the connection between the observer and the observed that is implicit in the formulations of quantum theory. For example, if our apparent separation from the objects we observe is merely an illusion of the explicate order, we are ultimately no more separate from them than adjacent designs on a piece of carpet. It is important to note that the apparent effect an observer has on the quantum system he or she is observing does not imply that some sort of causal interaction is taking place between the two. As Bohm states, one can thus "regard terms like 'observed object,' 'observing instrument,' 'link electron,' 'experimental results,' etc., as aspects of a single overall 'pattern' that are in effect abstracted or 'pointed out' by our mode of description. Thus, to speak of the interaction of 'observing instrument' and 'observed object' has no meaning."[7]

In short, if quantum particles are all projections of a deeper, nonlocal reality, such a state of affairs would force us to reassess many of our ideas about the physical world. Given that all objects that we know of are constructed out of quanta, from Sequoia trees to quasars, if Bohm's theory is correct, it means that all things in the universe are infinitely interconnected. Or as Bohm puts it, "Everything interpenetrates everything."[8] If such a point of view is correct, not only would it give new meaning to Blake's advice "to see a world in a grain of sand,'' but it would have many other profound implications as well.

## THE UNIVERSE AS A MULTIDIMENSIONAL HOLOGRAM

For centuries we have labored under the illusion that the universe is a gigantic machine, and that we can understand it by dismantling it. But if the universe is infinitely interconnected, there are certain phenomena—such as subatomic systems—for which this approach is no longer valid. Because of this Bohm concludes that the correlations between subatomic particles indicate that a revolutionary new understanding of order is at hand, one in which the universe should no longer be viewed as a machine but more properly as a stupendous multidimensional hologram.[9]

A hologram is a three-dimensional photograph manufactured with the aid of a laser. To make a hologram, scientists first shine a laser beam on an object and then bounce a second laser beam off the reflected light of the first. Interestingly, it is the pattern of interference created by the two lasers that is recorded on a piece of film to create a hologram. To the naked eye, the image recorded on such a piece of film is a meaningless swirl. However, if another laser beam is shown through the developed film, the image reappears in all of its original and three-dimensional glory.

In addition to being three-dimensional, the image recorded in a hologram differs from a conventional photograph in another very important way. If you cut a normal photograph in half, each section will contain only half of the image that was contained in the original photograph. This is because each tiny section of the photograph, like each dot on a color television, contains only a single bit of information about the entire image. However, if you cut a hologram in half and then shine a laser through one of the sections, you will find that each half still contains the entire image of the original hologram. Each tiny section of the hologram contains not only its own bit of information but every other bit of information from the rest of the image as well. Thus, you can cut a hologram up into pieces and each individual piece will still contain a blurrier but complete version of the entire picture. In other words, in a hologram, every part of the image interpenetrates every other part in the same way that Bohm's nonlocal universe would interpenetrate all of its parts.

If Bohm is correct and the universe is a gigantic multidimensional hologram, such an underlying holographic order would have profound implications for many of our other commonsense notions about reality. For example, in a holographic universe, time and space would no longer be viewed as fundamentals. Because the universe would be seen as possessing a deeper level in which concepts such as location break down, time and three-dimensional space, like the images of the fish on the television monitors, would have to be viewed as projections of this deeper order. In other words, in the superhologram of the universe, past present, and future are all enfolded and exist simultaneously. This suggests that it might even be possible to someday reach into the superhologram and retrieve from oblivion the long-forgotten past.[10]

Bohm discovered another metaphor for envisioning an enfolded order while watching a television science program in the 1960s. In the show, the narrator demonstrated an interesting phenomenon involving a drop of ink and a specially designed jar containing a rotating cylinder and a narrow space filled with glycerine. First the narrator placed a drop of ink in the cylinder. Then the narrator turned a handle which caused the cylinder and the glycerine surrounding it to smear into nothingness and become enfolded in the glycerine. However, when the handle was turned in the

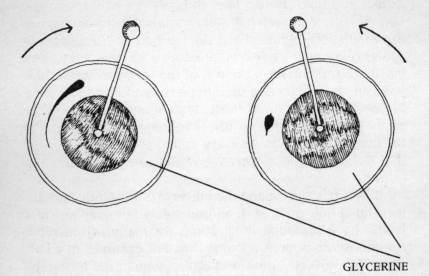

FIGURE 6    *When the crank is turned one way the drop of ink vanishes in the thick glycerine. When the crank is turned back the other way the drop of ink reappears.*

other direction, the original drop of ink reappeared as if it were unfolded from the glycerine and regained its original shape (see Figure 6). This gave Bohm a metaphor for exactly the sort of process he was conceptualizing.[11]

In terms of time, the universe as we perceive it, with its apparently separate succession of moments, would be the smear of ink once the turning handle has stretched it out into a long ribbon. We are not able to perceive that time, at the level of the superhologram, possesses a coherent and unbroken structure, because that structure is enfolded or implicate in the level of the universe that we are privy to. Time and three-dimensional space are not the only processes Bohm feels are best explained as enfoldings and unfoldings in and out of the implicate order.

## MIND CONNECTIONS

Perhaps the most intriguing aspect of Bohm's theory is how it might apply to our understanding of the human mind. As he sees it, if every particle of matter interconnects with every other particle, the brain itself must be viewed as infinitely interconnected with the rest of the universe. Bohm believes that such a mind-boggling interconnectedness might even shed light on the phenomenon of consciousness itself.

To begin with, one of the great unsolved puzzles of all time is the so-called mind-body problem. Simply stated, the mind-body problem can be summed up in a single question: Is there any fundamental difference between the mind and the body? This is just another way of saying, What is consciousness? Is consciousness simply the sum of what is going on in our brains, or is it something more, something that is fundamentally different from matter and thus perhaps capable of surviving the death of the physical body?

The standard answer of science is, of course, that there is no ultimate distinction between mind and body. Consciousness is synonymous with the brain, and when the brain dies all of those things that we associate with consciousness—self-awareness, perception, acts of understanding, and so on—die with it. The opposing point of view is that we are more than the sum of our parts and when we die some aspect of our consciousness survives and goes on. If we accept this point of view, the question then becomes, What is that something that survives?

One great thinker who articulated with unusual clarity what that something might be was the seventeenth-century French philosopher and mathematician, René Descartes. Descartes described matter as "extended substance." Evidently, by "extended substance" Descartes meant that matter is something that is made up of distinct forms and exists in space. In contrast to this he referred to consciousness as "thinking substance," and by drawing such a sharp distinction between the two, clearly implied that the various distinct forms that appear in thought do not have extensions or separations in space as we know it.

Bohm is particularly taken with this assessment and points out that Descartes' distinctions between consciousness and matter are precisely the same distinctions that he makes between the implicate and explicate order. Bohm is cautious, however, about jumping to conclusions. As he states, "It is difficult to say much about faculties as subtle as these."[12] However, Bohm does believe that by reflecting on and giving careful attention to what happens in certain experiences, one can obtain further valuable clues about the possible connection between consciousness and the implicate order.

Bohm suggests, for example, that one consider the process that goes on when one listens to a beautiful piece of music. At any given moment only a single note might be played, but somehow the mind connects each note into a sensation of wholeness. As Bohm sees it, one does not experience the actuality of the whole piece of music by holding onto the past or comparing any given note with one's memories of the previous notes. Rather, each note causes an *active transformation* of what came earlier. As Bohm states, "One can thus obtain a direct sense of how a sequence of notes is enfolding into many levels of consciousness, and of how at any given moment, the transformations flowing out of many such enfolded notes interpenetrate and intermingle to give rise to an immediate and primary feeling of movement."[13] Bohm further suggests that this is one way that each of us experiences firsthand the holographic or implicate nature of consciousness. This is not the only evidence available to us that suggests that consciousness might be holographic.

Working separately from Bohm, over the past decade, Stanford neurophysiologist Karl Pribram has also proposed

a holographic model of consciousness. To support his conclusion Pribram cites evidence that memory does not seem
to be stored in any particular localized part or individual cell
in the brain but instead somehow seems to be distributed
over the whole brain. One of the fundamental achievements
in neurophysiology has been the discovery of direct relationships between certain locations in the brain and specific
body functions—speech centers, visual centers, and so on.
However, as far back as the 1920s, neurophysiologist Karl
Lashley discovered that partial damage to the brain did not
prevent a person from performing functions controlled
by the missing parts. When one of the localized areas was
destroyed, it disrupted functions of the sense organs it
controlled; however, Lashley discovered that higher-level
functioning, such as memory of specific events, was not disturbed. Today neurophysiologists such as Pribram interpret
this phenomenon as proof that the structures responsible for
memorizing and remembering things are not located in any
single part of the brain but are distributed over the brain as
a whole in much the same way that the image of a hologram
is enfolded in all of its parts.[14]

Pribram is very intrigued with the fact that, starting from
a different point, Bohm has reached a similar conclusion. In
commenting on Bohm's work, Pribram hypothesizes that
perhaps the fuzziness of reality at the subatomic level is no
more haphazard or random than the meaningless swirl the
naked eye perceives in a hologram before a laser is shone
through it. Pribram goes on to postulate that perhaps even
at a level available to our perceptions, objective reality is
holographic and might be thought of as little more than a
"frequency domain." That is, even the world we know may
not be composed of objects. We may only be sensing mechanisms moving through a vibrating dance of frequencies.
Pribram suggests that the reason we translate this vibrating
dance of frequencies into the solidity and objectivity of the
universe as we know it is that our brains operate on the

same holographiclike principles as the dance of frequencies and is able to convert them into a picture much the same as a television converts the frequencies it receives into a more coherent image.

To support his hypothesis that our perceptual systems operate according to frequencies, Pribram points out that there is indisputable evidence that our visual systems are also sensitive to sound waves. It is suggested that only in the holographic domain of the consciousness are these sorted out and divided up into conventional perceptions. Indeed, Pribram notes that even at the cellular level both animals and humans are sensitive to a broad range of frequencies that we do not necessarily translate into perceptions. He concludes that we are neither creating nor merely receiving reality. As he puts it, "I think the brain generates its own constructions and images of physical reality. But at the same time it generates them in such a way that they resonate with what really is there."[15]

Bohm believes that even life itself has aspects of an implicate order written all over it. For example, according to conventional biological understanding, a seed contains within it very little of the actual material substance that will ultimately be contained in the plant that it becomes. Most of the substance of the plant comes from the soil, water, air, and sunlight. According to modern theories, what the seed does contain is *information*, in the form of DNA, and somehow it is this information that directs the environment to form a corresponding plant.

However, as the plant is formed, maintained, and dissolved by the exchange of matter and energy with its environment, at what point can we say that there is a sharp distinction between what is alive and what is not? Similarly, when a molecule of carbon dioxide suddenly crosses a cell boundary into a leaf, it does not suddenly come alive. Nor does a molecule of oxygen suddenly die when the leaf expels it into the atmosphere. As Bohm sees it, this lack of distinct boundaries between what is alive and what is not once again underscores the inadequacy of a strictly mechanistic approach to the universe. Instead of trying to divide the universe into parts that are alive and parts that are not, a better approach might be to view the universe as an unbroken whole, a totality into which both living and nonliving things are constantly enfolding and unfolding.

It might be said that right now, in the soil, air, and water, there is an ensemble of atoms that will eventually become a plant. In the standard view it cannot properly be said that they are alive, but in Bohm's view it might be that the order that we recognize as living order is already implicit within them, enfolded in the superhologram of reality just as the order we recognize as a drop of ink is already enfolded in the smear of glycerine.

What does all of this make of the mind-body problem? As Bohm sees it, if the universe is nonlocal at a subquantum level, that means that reality is ultimately a seamless web, and it is only our own idiosyncrasies that direct us to divide it up into such arbitrary categories as mind and body. Thus, consciousness cannot be considered as fundamentally separate from matter, any more than life can be considered as fundamentally separate from nonlife. There is no dualism because both are secondary and derivative categories and both are enfolded in a higher common ground.

This ultimate lack of division between the two, Bohm asserts, may lead to still further reassessments of ourselves and our role in the universe. For example, if the universe is holographic and each human brain interpenetrates every other human brain (indeed, every other particle in the universe), on some level that is beyond ordinary subjective experience, the human race may really be one organism. As to whether this interconnectedness might produce phenomena resembling ESP, Bohm is very cautious. As he states, "Different people who are somehow attuned to each other might develop common notions at the same time. This would be almost indistinguishable from what we would mean by telepathy."[16] In fact, Bohm believes that if the paranormal exists, "it can only be understood through reference to the implicate order, since in that order everything contacts everything else and thus there is no intrinsic reason why the paranormal should be impossible."[17]

However, Bohm does believe that it might someday be possible for people to perceive the higher and multidimensional common ground where consciousness and matter are no longer separate and in essence become a sort of group mind. Where or how this higher ground may be perceived, Bohm does not know and says only that it is a "deeper and more inward actuality" that is "neither mind nor body but rather a yet higher-dimensional actuality."[18] Bohm cannot say how many dimensions this higher actuality might possess; however, he boldly suggests that at the superholographic level the universe may have as many dimensions as there are subatomic particles in our three-dimensional universe, a staggering $10^{89}$. And even then, Bohm asserts, this superholographic level may still be a "mere stage" beyond which is "an infinity of further development."[19]

What other characteristics might typify such a higher, multidimensional common ground? Bohm cautiously states, "It is vast, rich, and in a state of unending flux of enfoldment and unfoldment, with laws most of which are only vaguely known."[20] However, he then goes on to add that because consciousness and matter, life and nonlife, are all one in this common ground, the totality itself must be seen as possessing these qualities. In other words, nature itself must be viewed as a living organism, and given the diversity and richness of forms that the superhologram perpetually pours forth, it is even safe to conclude that it is "purposive" and possesses "deep intentionality." All of the creativity and insight that we ourselves experience must also be seen as derivative of this common ground, and thus in a sense it seems that nature has made us seek her. Perhaps that is why there is a deep drive in all of us to understand the universe. It would no longer be correct to speak of the multidimensional level of the universe as a material plane. Rather, Bohm concludes, "it could equally well be called Idealism, Spirit, Consciousness. The separation of the two— matter and spirit—is an abstraction. The ground is always one."[21]

Reaction to Bohm's views is varied. Some, like physicist Terry Clark of the University of Sussex, speak of Bohm with unabashed awe: "Bohm has been an inspiration to us kids in trying to break out of these closed philosophical views the Bohr school set up in the 1920s and 1930s."[22]

Many scientists are critical of Bohm's views. Boston University physicist Abner Shimony says, "You have to give the man tremendous respect and a long leash because of his important accomplishments in physics, but when you try very hard to understand his ideas and still can't, you just have to go by your own judgement."[23] Shimony's criticism of Bohm is that he has not yet ironed out the mathematics of his theory. Others argue that Bohm's ideas are not yet experimentally testable, which is the bottom line for any scientific theory.

Bohm, however, remains optimistic. Throughout his book he emphasizes that his theory is still very much in progress, and the mathematics supporting it only tentative. And just as methods were devised which ultimately allowed the Einstein-Podolsky-Rosen conjecture to be tested, techniques will be developed to enable researchers to prove or disprove his own speculations about the existence of a subquantum reality.

The vast majority of physicists, however, pay no attention to Bohm's work because they hold fast to their conviction that nothing lies beyond the quantum. They reject it out of hand. Because human science is gripped by the Limit Syndrome, and because we have not yet encountered instantaneous communication between objects divided by space and time, the current wisdom holds that instantaneous communication can never occur. This, then, is one of the most important lessons to be learned from Bohm's work —not necessarily the specific details of his theory, but the fact that he is a dissenting voice and one of the few physicists of his stature brave enough to risk his reputation on a conviction that there is more going on in the subatomic realm than current theory yet explains.

A second important message in Bohm's work is his suggestion that to fully comprehend the phenomena of the subatomic world we must begin to embrace an entirely new understanding of order. That understanding involves switching from the mechanical to the holographic, or the view that on occasion significant aspects of a phenomenon may be understood less by examining its parts and more by examining a totality or wholeness that is perhaps greater than the sum of its parts. As we will see, suggestions of this new sense of order are popping up in other branches of science as well.

Quantum physics is not the only field in which unsolved puzzles are leading some researchers to postulate the existence of levels of reality that science has yet to penetrate and describe. Recently, a Cambridge biochemist named Rupert Sheldrake called attention to similar puzzles in biology which will be the subject of the next chapter. Sheldrake believes that these unsolved puzzles can only be explained by postulating the existence of a new type of field as yet unrecognized by any science. Even more important, unlike Bohm, Sheldrake has formulated his theory in a manner that is experimentally testable, and tests have already been run with results suggesting that Sheldrake may be right.

# 3

# The Wavelength of Life

> When Rupert Sheldrake's book *A New Science of Life*
> came out in England in 1981 . . . letters poured in.
> They still do, and they are mostly favorable to the
> new idea. And, to even the most scientifically back-
> ward of people, the possibilities are intriguing be-
> yond words.
>
> —MICHAEL KERNAN, *The Washington Post*

IS IT EASIER for children living today to learn how to play
video games than it was for children a few years ago? Will
adults of the next generation automatically be able to understand and operate computers faster than people learning
how to operate them today? The answer to these questions,
says Rupert Sheldrake, just might be *yes*. Just as the mechanistic approach fails to account for certain subatomic
phenomena, Sheldrake believes it also leaves a number of
disturbing and unsolved puzzles in his own field of biology.
To explain these, Sheldrake proposes the existence of a new
kind of field, a mysterious force that he says connects each
individual with all other individuals in its species' past.
Sheldrake further suggests that each species has a "group
mind" that may provide a scientific basis for understanding
certain psychic phenomena as well.

The path that ultimately led Sheldrake to formulate his
theory is similar in certain respects to the situation that confronted Bohm. In biology, as in quantum physics, the orthodox view is that phenomena such as living organisms are

57

nothing more than complex machines, governed only by the known laws of physics and chemistry. However, even as an undergraduate at Cambridge, Sheldrake became troubled with what he perceived as problems that could not be explained by this approach.

Foremost among these is the problem of *morphogenesis*. The word "morphogenesis" comes from the Greek term *morphe*, meaning "form," and *genesis*, meaning "birth." Thus the problem of morphogenesis is the mystery of how living forms come into being. For example, we know from the mechanistic approach that the DNA in each of our cells contains the coded information that describes how all of the proteins in our body are put together. It is the conventional wisdom in science that the DNA can therefore be thought of as a blueprint.

What science does not know is what directs this blueprint to make the decisions that it seems to make. It is important to note that the genetic blueprint in the cells that constitute any given organism are exactly the same. For example, when a fertilized egg first begins to develop into a fetus, the cells composing it are undifferentiated. However, as the cell mass continues to divide, the cells gradually begin to align themselves in a way that produces an embryo; certain cells become heart cells, while certain other cells become brain cells. The question is, How does a cell know what it should become? How does a heart cell know to read only the information off of the DNA that tells it how to become a heart cell?

Think about this for a moment. Imagine that in an empty lot you come upon a pile of building materials and on each and every piece of lumber is a tiny list of all the materials that will ultimately constitute the house. Imagine that as you watch, the lumber, the nails, the roofing tiles, and the doorknobs all begin to assemble themselves into the structure of the house. The question is, What force allows all of the building materials to read the blueprint, discern their own special niche out of thousands of possibilities, and then align themselves into a house? This is one of the problems of morphogenesis.

Another problem of morphogenesis concerns a phenomenon biologists call "regulation." Regulation is the ability of a developing organism to alter or regulate its own design if something unexpected happens to its original plan of development. For example, suppose a dragonfly egg is tied around its middle shortly after it is laid, dividing in half the mass of undifferentiated cells that will ultimately grow into a dragonfly. Instead of developing into half a dragonfly, the remaining mass will regulate itself and develop into a smaller but complete dragonfly (see Figure 7). The same thing happens in human beings, which is why, if a cell mass is divided at a certain stage of its development, identical twins are born and not partial humans.

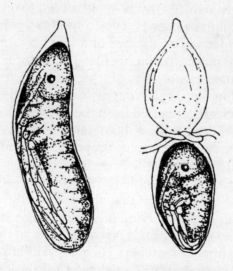

FIGURE 7   *An example of regulation. On the left is a normal dragonfly embryo and on the right are two small but complete embryos formed after their egg was tied in half soon after being laid (after Weiss, 1939).*

What is intriguing about the ability of living organisms to regulate themselves in this manner is that this is once again parallel to properties we have come to expect from a hologram. Just as each half of a hologram contains a complete version of the original image, so each half of a developing assemblage of cells contains a complete version of the original organism enfolded within it. The current mechanistic approach to biology has no explanation for this phenomenon.

A third unexplained problem of morphogenesis has to do with regeneration, the ability of many organisms to replace or restore damaged areas. If a newt loses a leg, it can quickly grow a new one. If a starfish is broken into pieces, each piece can grow into a new starfish. Sometimes the ability of a creature to regenerate is so phenomenal that it does not even seem that it can be explained as a product of natural selection. For example, around the turn of the century a biologist named Gustav Wolff set out to test the regenerative capabilities of newts. To accomplish this he surgically removed the lens from the eye of a newt in a manner that could not have occurred accidentally in nature. Under normal circumstances the lens of a developing newt embryo grows out of its skin, but Wolff discovered in his experiment that a new lens regenerated from the newt's iris.[1]

Once again, as with a hologram, it seems that living organisms possess a curious property of wholeness. The conventional view is that the mechanistic approach will ultimately explain these problems. However, a growing number of researchers believe that the apparently holographic processes that occur in living organisms suggest that a new understanding of order must be considered. In the last chapter we saw how researchers such as Pribram and Bohm believe that a holographic model must be considered in such disparate fields as the study of memory and the study of subatomic systems. What we shall see now is that the remarkable properties possessed by such holographic systems are very similar to another widely occurring natural phenomenon.

## MORPHOGENETIC FIELDS

As every child learns in science class, if you place a sheet of paper over a bar magnet and sprinkle iron filings over the top of it, the filings tend to align themselves in the curved lines of what physicists call the magnet's electromagnetic field. The world, physicists tell us, is interpenetrated with a variety of fields. What are these fields? Physicists often answer that fields are mathematical quantities that manifest in regions of space. Or, as in the case of a gravitational field, they are a geometric property of space, or they are curved space. Although we know a great deal about the way fields affect the world as we perceive it, the truth is no one really knows what a field is. The closest we can come to describing what they are is to say that they are spatial structures in the fabric of space itself.

Our ignorance notwithstanding, one of the things we do know about fields is that, like holograms, they also possess a mysterious propensity toward wholeness. For example, if you have a bar magnet beneath a sheet of paper covered with iron filings, you will see that the lines of force in the magnet's electromagnetic field will circle out from one of the magnet's poles, and connect with the other. However, if you break the magnet in half, the pattern of the iron filings does not also break in half, but instantly reorganizes itself to once again form two complete fields (see Figure 8).

This similarity between what goes on in fields and in living organisms is one of the things that caused Sheldrake to propose that the problems encountered in morphogenesis might be explained by the existence of an unknown type of field, what Sheldrake called a "morphogenetic field," or "M-field" for short.

This idea is by no means new. In the 1920s, two em-

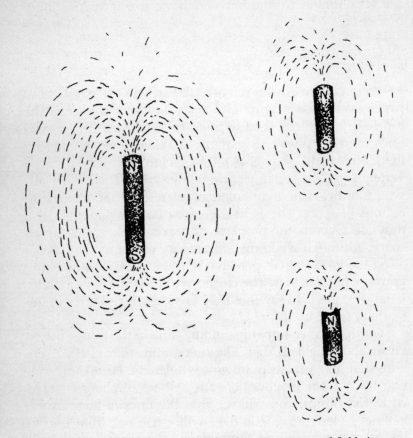

FIGURE 8   *An example of the self-organizing aspect of fields in general. Even when a magnet is broken in half, it will always have a north and a south pole and its field will be smaller but complete.*

bryologists, Alexander Gurwitsch and Paul Weiss, each advanced theories about morphogenetic fields. However, apart from stating that the control of morphogenesis might be due to morphogenetic fields, neither Gurwitsch nor Weiss went on to specify what such fields were or how they worked, and their theories became little more than footnotes in the annals of biology.

Now, in addition to resurrecting the idea of morphogenetic fields, Sheldrake has also fleshed out the hypothesis more fully. He asserts that morphogenctic fields govern not only the structure of living organisms but their behavior as well. In short, what Sheldrake proposes is that the habits and behavior of any given species in the past builds up and, through a process he calls "morphic resonance," affects the habits and behavior of members of the same species living today. For example, if a lion found a new hunting technique that proved unusually successful and a sufficient number of its fellow lions also learned the technique, morphic resonance might allow lions in completely separate geographic areas to suddenly absorb the technique in spite of the fact that they had no direct genetic connection to the lions who originated the technique.

Evidence of morphic resonance, Sheldrake says, can still be found around us today. In his 1981 book *A New Science of Life*, he cites the anomalous experimental results encountered by Harvard psychologist William McDougall in his studies of rat behavior. McDougall began his test in the 1920s and continued them over a 34-year period. His original intention was to test Jean Lamarck's famous theory that acquired characteristics can be passed on genetically.

To conduct his tests McDougall constructed a T-shaped water maze. At one end of the T-shaped maze he placed a light and at the other he placed an opaque roof so that it remained dark. He then electrified the gangway at the lighted end. He did this because he knew that the rat's natural inclination would be to swim toward the lighted gangway and he wanted to see how many times it would take them to learn that only the dark gangway provided safe access out.

To McDougall's astonishment what he discovered was that later generations of rats kept completing the maze more quickly than preceding generations. To determine whether this increase in learning was being encoded in the rats' genes, he even bred only the slowest learning rats in each generation, but still the increase in learning persisted. The effect was so marked that McDougall discovered his twenty-second generation of rats were figuring the maze out ten times faster than his first generation had (see Figure 9). Even more disarming, McDougall discovered that rats from un-trained genetic lines displayed the same rate of improvement. In other words, the improvement seemed to manifest in the rat species en masse, disproving the idea that the increase was Lamarckian, or being passed on genetically.

One of McDougall's critics, a Scottish researcher named F.A.E. Crew, set out to disprove McDougall's results, because he did not believe they were possible. To Crew's surprise, the knowledge his rats seemed to possess about the maze started up where McDougall's rats left off. Furthermore, whereas McDougall's first generation of rats had required hundreds of immersions before they learned to successfully negotiate the maze, some of Crew's rats learned the task immediately, without being shocked at all. Following this, an Australian researcher named W. E. Agar initiated a similar series of experiments and continued them for twenty-five years, with equally disconcerting results.[2] The rats in both Crew's and Agar's studies were from completely separate genetic lines than those used by McDougall, again demonstrating that the skill could not have been passed on genetically.

Conventional science holds that such anomalies mean nothing and should be ignored. Most biologists believe that acquired traits can only be passed on genetically, and thus if there is no genetic connection between the groups of rats in McDougall's, Crew's, and Agar's experiments, there cannot possibly be any connection between their similar and bizarre behavior. This is not to say that orthodox biology embraces Lamarckism. On the contrary, thousands of exhaustive studies have turned up no convincing evidence that a behavior learned by a parent organism can become encoded in the

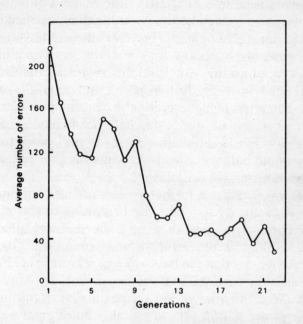

FIGURE 9    *The average number of errors in successive generations of rats (data from McDougall, 1938).*

genetic material it passes on to its descendants. As for how behaviors such as instincts become genetically incorporated into a species, very little is understood. The conventional explanation is that they are not learned and then passed on, but simply appear, spontaneously and randomly, and because they are useful, they tend to survive in the great sieve of natural selection.

Sheldrake believes that findings such as McDougall's suggest an alternative explanation. As he sees it, each species has its own M-field, which, like the fields spoken of in physics, are intangible but real spatial structures. The M-field of a rat, for instance, would have encoded within it (perhaps holographically) all of the structure and behavior that we presently perceive in rats. The developing rat embryo would tune into or share in the M-field of its species. However, as suggested by the McDougall experiment, these fields are not stable or static, but can allow a new and beneficial behavior—such as a rat's learning to swim a maze—to be *fed back* into the M-field of the organism. Instead of all learned behavior being lost when an individual dies and all inborn behavior being merely the result of random and spontaneous genetic mutation, habitual behavior and nature's random and innovative forces would work together in a dynamic balance. Sheldrake calls his theory the "hypothesis of formative causation."

Sheldrake makes a further assault on conventional biological wisdom. As stated at the beginning of this chapter, science currently accepts that the DNA of an organism contains a biological blueprint of that organism. However, Sheldrake asserts that we have no real reason to believe that even this is the case. All that we know with certainty is that the DNA contains the coded recipes for all the proteins of living organisms. But, says Sheldrake, no one has yet demonstrated that the DNA also contains the design of an organism—no one has isolated a strand of DNA, for example, and shown that it contains the directions for making an eyeball or a human hand. Thus, says Sheldrake, to say that the DNA contains the blueprint of an organism is to make a conceptual leap that we currently do not have the right to make. If his hypothesis is correct, it may be that the DNA is little more than a list of ingredient formulas.

To better visualize how an M-field might function in relation to the physical biology of an organism, Sheldrake offers the metaphor of a television. Imagine a man who previously has never seen a television trying to explain how it works. If he had no knowledge of electromagnetic radiation he might imagine that the pictures appearing on the screen are purely the product of the television's internal components. If he started to take the television apart, this theory would be proven, for he would quickly discover that any alterations he made on the television's circuits would affect the picture. Sheldrake feels that biologists are currently in the same situation as the man with the television. They believe that form and behavior are completely encoded in the genes (the television's hardware) and have completely overlooked the fact that morphogenetic fields (the wave transmissions that the television is receiving) might also be integral to explaining the television's operation.

One of the most disconcerting implications of such a notion, however, is that for the M-fields of an organism in the past to be able to influence the behavior and form of an organism in the present and future, one must conclude that M-fields are also able to instantaneously cut across both space and time. To make this assertion seem less daunting, Sheldrake suggests that perhaps a new view of time is also in order. We usually think of time as being stretched out like space. If a year is viewed as one unit long, we tend to view something that occurred fifty years in the past as stretched out fifty units behind us. Sheldrake suggests that perhaps the past is "pressed up against" us, or "collapsed immediately behind" us, an idea remarkably like Bohm's idea of an enfolded universe. Thus, any part of the past might be far more accessible to us than we have previously imagined.[3]

Because of theoretical similarities such as these, Bohm was asked in a recent interview if he felt there was a relationship between his concept of the implicate order and Sheldrake's M-field theory. He replied:

The major difference is that the implicate order is more general. It does not require morphogenetic theory, but it may have room to explain one. . . . The implicate order can be thought of as a ground beyond time, a totality out of which each moment is projected into the explicate order. For every moment that is projected out into the explicate there would be another movement in which that moment would be injected or "introjected" back into the implicate order. Now, if you have a large number of repetitions of this process, you'll start to build up a fairly constant component to this series of projection and injection. That is, a fixed disposition would become established. The point is that, via this process, past forms would tend to be repeated or replicated in the present, and that is very similar to what Sheldrake calls a morphogenetic field and a morphic resonance.[4]

Because M-fields would have the ability to cut across both space and time, Sheldrake believes that they would therefore have to be "non-energetic," or able to cause effects without involving any transfer of energy. Bohm does not feel that this is necessarily the case. He likes Sheldrake's metaphor of an organism being like a television receiver, but he points out that what such a metaphor really implies is that there are two levels of energy. One is unformed but is subject to being formed by very tiny impulses. The other is a field that is much more subtle and has very little energy in the usual sense of the word, "but has a quality of form which can be taken up by the energy of the [television] receiver. . . . The point is that one might look at the implicate order that way; the subtler levels of the implicate order are affecting the energy in the less subtle levels. The implicate energies are very fine; they would not ordinarily even be counted as energies. . . ."[5] Bohm goes on to say that the subtle energies involved in M-fields may be very similar to the subtle energies he feels allow subatomic particles to communicate with each other nonlocally, regardless of separation in space and time.[6]

Sheldrake provides further evidence to support his hypothesis. In a recent experiment conducted by biologist Mae Wan Ho and colleagues at the Open University at Walton, England, Ho's team took fruit fly eggs from an ordinary stock and exposed them to ether. Such exposure caused some of the fruit flies hatched from the eggs to develop two sets of wings instead of one. In the first generation of exposed flies Ho discovered that four percent developed double sets of wings and 96 percent remained normal. After letting these flies mate at random, the researchers exposed the next generation of eggs to ether, and in this generation they found that about 8 percent developed double sets of wings. They continued the procedure, and to their astonishment they discovered that in each succeeding generation of fruit flies, more and more were born with mutations—10 percent, 12 percent, and so on, until the team reached a point where 40 or 50 percent of a generation was showing up with double wings.

Ho and her colleagues concluded that this might be due to some sort of Lamarckian effect. However, they subsequently discovered that after being exposed to ether, even 10 percent of all fruit fly eggs from the regular stock in their laboratory—flies whose genetic ancestors had never been exposed to ether—developed double wings! In the next generation they found 20 percent. Even assuming the existence of some sort of genetic influence, such an effect should not have occurred in a completely unrelated population of fruit flies.[7]

Sheldrake believes that the existence of M-fields might explain other phenomena as well. One of these is the striking parallels we find in organisms that have followed widely divergent paths of evolution. In Australia, for example, marsupial versions of dogs, mice, flying squirrels, and so on have evolved that are similar to their placental cousins on other continents. In Sheldrake's view, although organisms tend to hook into the M-field of their own species, it is conceivable that organisms could also tune into useful innovations in the M-fields of more distantly related organisms.

This might explain many of the other puzzling similarities we find in living things. Although it would seem that in the random hurly-burly of evolution all possible shapes and sizes of organisms should arise, this is not entirely the case. When we look at different varieties of land vertebrates from widely different ages and environments we find that most of them have four legs. It might be argued that four-leggedness is the optimal design for running on land, but that would not explain why fish, the ancestors of terrestrial animals, also have four limbs, or fins. The standard biological answer is simply to admit that evolution, in certain ways, seems to be a remarkably conservative affair. But no explanation for this natural conservatism is currently known. According to Sheldrake's hypothesis, however, such conservatism is the result of morphic resonance and thus is merely the product of habit. The fact that nature has done something one way tends to make her do it that way again, and the more this duplication is repeated, the more powerful the M-field becomes.

The theory also predicts that organisms living today may be able to hook into the M-fields of similar organisms in the remote past. Sheldrake believes that the ability of a species to tune into such fossil M-fields may explain a biological phenomenon known as atavism, or the reversion of an organism to a more ancestral form. For example, if one examines the literature on teratology, the study of biological monstrosities and malformations, one finds numerous instances of such atavistic anomalies as children born with tails and even gill slits, and insects born with extra segments like their more primitive ancestors. Even the four-winged fruit flies in Ho's experiment may be examples of atavism in that they resemble a similar four-winged ancestor of the fruit fly that lived many millions of years ago.

## THE M-FIELDS OF INANIMATE OBJECTS

Living organisms are not the only things that are controlled by M-fields, according to Sheldrake. For years, crystallographers have noticed an unusual phenomenon that may best be explained by Sheldrake's M-field hypothesis. That is, when a new chemical substance is crystallized for the first time, it doesn't immediately know what crystalline shape to grow into. It flounders around for a bit and then after a while settles upon a structure. From that point on, all over the world, whenever the substance is crystallized it always assumes that shape.

In their 1961 book, *Crystals and Crystal Growing*, Alan Holden and Phylis Singer relate an incident that occurred in the early 1950s at a company involved in growing single large crystals of a chemical known as ethylene diamine tartrate. For three years the company was unable to develop a type of crystal known as the monohydrate form. They discovered, however, that another crystalline form of the substance known as the anhydrous form was relatively easy to manufacture and settled for that variety instead. They produced these in great numbers and then shipped them off to another factory where they would be readied for industrial use.

A year after the company began performing this procedure, the crystals in their growing tanks suddenly started to grow misshapen. After running several tests, company officials discovered that they were producing the monohydrate form they had previously tried so desperately to create. Moreover, monohydrate forms of the crystal started to appear everywhere, even growing on crystals at the other factory.

Because of the frequency with which this phenomenon occurs, Holden and Singer go so far as to suggest that different planets possess different dominant crystal forms. They add, "Perhaps in our own world many other possible solid species are still unknown, not because their ingredients are lacking, but simply because suitable seeds have not yet put in an appearance."[8]

The usual explanation for this occurrence is that microscopic seed crystals travel through the air and infect other crystals. Sheldrake concedes that this is a likely explanation when such incidents occur over short range. However, he points out that there are numerous incidents of new crystalline forms appearing all at once in similar industrial processes around the world. Again he concedes that these could be due to microscopic seed crystals traveling through the air, but he finds such an explanation implausible. Instead, he suggests that each crystalline form is also controlled by its own M-field and that this is why the repetition of a new form seems to make it easier and easier to reproduce. Importantly, Sheldrake points out that the seed theory for such phenomena should be a relatively easy proposition to test experimentally, and that if it is disproved this would lend support to his own hypothesis.

## THE SOCIAL IMPLICATIONS OF M-FIELDS

The most intriguing aspect of Sheldrake's M-field theory is, of course, its impact on our lives. The most obvious social implication is that thoughts and behaviors that become habitual in sufficient numbers of people—whether beneficial to the human race or not—would become increasingly easier for other individuals to tune into. This has come to be referred to as the "hundredth monkey effect."

This term was first coined by biologist Lyall Watson in his 1979 book, *Lifetide*. In that book, Watson relates an unusual incident that allegedly occurred in the 1950s in a population of Japanese monkeys known as *Macaca fuscata* on the island of Koshima just off the east coast of Kyushu. It seems that while studying the local population of these monkeys, researchers started feeding them sweet potatoes and would dump truckloads of them on the beach for the monkeys to retrieve. The problem was that although the monkeys had developed elaborate feeding habits for all of their indigenous foods, they had never seen sweet potatoes before. Their dilemma was not that they did not like the new treat, but that the sweet potatoes were covered with sand and grit—an unpleasant problem that the monkeys had never before confronted.

As Watson tells the story, the monkeys struggled with

the problem for a while, like picnickers assailed by ants, and then an eighteen-month-old female, a sort of monkey genius the researchers knew as Imo, solved the dilemma. Imo discovered that if the gritty sweet potatoes were dunked in the ocean, not only did it remove the sand, but it added an interesting new flavor. Imo next taught the trick to her mother, then her playmates, and slowly the new habit gained a small following in the Koshima colony.

Then something remarkable transpired. As Watson relates, the details of what happened next have not yet been published because the primate researchers involved knew that what they would be disclosing was too heretical for general scientific consumption. It seems that one morning the number of monkeys that had learned Imo's washing technique reached a sort of critical mass, and then, suddenly, by that evening, every monkey in the colony was washing potatoes in the surf. Not only that, but researchers reported that troops of monkeys on other islands and even a troop on the mainland at Takasakiyama also suddenly and spontaneously began practicing Imo's washing technique. Although the researchers on Koshima had not observed at precisely what number of monkeys this critical mass was reached, for the sake of speaking about it Watson refers to the monkey individual that put the entire population over the threshold as the proverbial "hundredth monkey."[9]

Because of the anecdotal nature of the account, Sheldrake cautions against invoking the incident as proof positive of his M-field hypothesis, but he does predict that such an occurrence is possible, and he acknowledges that the hundredth monkey anecdote provides a good way for people to begin to visualize what he is talking about. It is also interesting to note that some nuclear disarmament groups are beginning to cite the hundredth monkey effect in their literature as evidence that sociopolitical movements that start out small may reach a similar critical mass and suddenly inspire a cultural transition in the entire population.

The bottom line of the hundredth monkey effect is that each species can be thought of as possessing a sort of group mind. Sheldrake suggests that the best evidence for the existence of such a group mind may be found in social insects such as termites. The South African biologist Eugène Marais has also posited that termites seem to function as if they possess such a group mind. To test his hypothesis, Marais put metal plates through nests to prevent any kind of communication between the termites, and found that as two termites set out to construct a new tunnel from opposite starting points, they still met at precisely the same point on opposite sides of the plates. Sheldrake cautions that the possibility remains that the termites might have been signaling each other by tapping on the metal plates, and so further tests must be done to rule out this possibility.

Similarly, entomologists have observed that when experimenters damage the nests of potter wasps, the wasps sometimes call upon skills to repair the breakage that are not employed during the normal building of their nests. This is similar in a strange way to the fact that the regenerative capabilities of organisms such as newts allow them to repair cellular damage in ways that are not normally called upon during the course of evolution.[10]

The hundredth monkey effect may explain certain human capabilities as well. For example, human children show a remarkable facility for learning language. Linguist Noam Chomsky proposes that our ability to acquire language, as well as an entire range of cognitive skills including our ability to interact socially, and our ability to analyze the personalities of others, may be genetically inherited.

Chomsky postulates that these skills developed in much the same way as the physical organs of the body developed. However, according to current thinking, this means that all of the intricate complexities that we know of as language acquisition developed as the result of an almost incomprehensible series of propitious accidents, random genetic mutations that bit by bit resulted in the formidable cognitive skills that we possess today. According to Sheldrake's hypothesis, instead of being genetic accidents that amassed in thousands of different and often disconnected genetic lines, such advances in cognitive skills could have been the innovations of a few individuals which, like Imo's potato washing technique, then spread through the entire species collectively.

Similarly, Sheldrake believes that if his M-field hypothesis is proven correct, it may go a long way toward explaining Carl Jung's notion of a collective unconscious, as well as leading to very different interpretations of phenomena in parapsychology, such as telepathy.

## EVIDENCE OF M-FIELDS BEING CREATED TODAY

Sheldrake believes that there are many examples of M-fields being created today. When the behaviorist B. F. Skinner first started performing his now famous pigeon experiments, he had to put the pigeons through a lengthy training period to even begin to get them to peck at lighted panels in his "Skinner boxes." However, modern researchers find that such lengthy training procedures are no longer necessary, and that pigeons show an immediate inclination to peck at the lighted panels—an anomaly that is only casually mentioned in current papers as evidence that perhaps previous researchers simply didn't notice how easy it is to get pigeons to perform the task.[11]

In the human world, James Flynn of New Zealand's University of Otago recently pointed out that American children are getting better and better at taking IQ tests. Going back through a series of old tests, Flynn discovered that the IQ of the average American child has risen 0.36 points per year since 1947 (a fact not immediately apparent because every year IQ tests are "normed" so that the average sample of the population will always score 100). To support his findings Flynn took old IQ tests and tried them on modern-day children, and the results plainly showed that the older the test, the easier the children found them.[12] Sheldrake does not necessarily think that this means we are becoming more intelligent; rather he believes it indicates that an M-field for taking IQ tests is building up in the human race, and that succeeding generations of children are getting better at taking them.

What is important about findings such as these, aside from corroborating Sheldrake's M-field hypothesis, is that they also point out a way that the theory can be tested. Sheldrake suggests that playing video games might offer a possible testing ground. In such a test, a population would be needed where video games are not as widespread as they are in the United States—for instance, in India. A group of children in Bombay would play a certain game and then their rate of learning would be measured. Six months later, a second group of children of similar age, education, and background would be chosen in another part of India, and tested to determine their rate of learning. If the M-field hypothesis is correct, the children in the second group should learn to play the game faster than the children in the first group.

Intrigued by the idea of undertaking such an experiment, in October 1982 the scientific periodical *New Scientist* offered a cash prize to any of their readers who could come up with the best test for Sheldrake's hypothesis. Since then a number of studies have taken place and have yielded consistently positive results in favor of Sheldrake's hypothesis. However, all have had aspects that critics say render the results ambiguous. One of the most recent experiments undertaken and designed to safeguard against these criticisms involves a set of abstract puzzle pictures that contain hidden images that only become apparent after one has stared at them for a while (see Figures 10 and 11).

According to Sheldrake's theory, the more people who learn to decipher the hidden images—devised by Morgan Sendall—the easier it will be for others to decipher them. In November 1984 the BBC obliged Sheldrake by airing the puzzle pictures on a television show viewed by an estimated 80 million people. Meanwhile, associates of Sheldrake all over the world were showing the picture to subjects who had never seen them before. As Sheldrake predicted, of the 6,500 individuals tested, those who saw the pictures after they were viewed by 80 million people in Britain found them slightly easier to decode than those who were confronted with the pictures before the broadcast.

As with Bohm's ideas, most mainstream biologists hotly dispute Sheldrake's hypothesis. When his book first appeared in England, a reviewer for the British scientific periodical *Nature* wrote, "This infuriating tract . . . is the best candidate for burning there has been for many years." However, some scientists have rushed to Sheldrake's defense. University of Glasgow philosopher Stephen Clark, for one, observes, "*Nature*'s contempt for [Sheldrake's] work is contempt for a whole, lively tradition of puzzlement and creative thought."[13] Sir Eric Ashby, botanist and former vice-chancellor of Cambridge, finds Sheldrake's theory "an astonishing challenge to orthodox theories of plant and animal development."[14] And a reviewer for *New Scientist* wrote, "Whether or not one agrees with [Sheldrake's] proposals . . . it is quite clear that one is dealing here with an important scientific inquiry into the nature of biological and physical reality."[15]

In answer to the many scientists opposing his ideas, Sheldrake notes that very few of them have actually read his book or offered any criticisms of the specific details of his hypothesis. In my own discussions with scientists I have

FIGURE 10 *Two images specially devised by Morgan Sendall for Sheldrake's television experiment. Somewhere in each set of patterns is a hidden image. (Solutions on page 80.)*

78

found this to be very much the case. Time and again when I
asked various biologists and physicists how they felt about
Sheldrake's work, they would passionately denounce it. But
when I asked them why they rejected it so emphatically, the
replies were seldom more specific than "because it's nonsense." One individual, a leading biologist, said she rejected
his work because "Sheldrake wants to throw out everything
else we know about molecular biology." This, of course, is
not true. As Sheldrake responds, "The M-field theory
doesn't deny the importance of DNA or conventional ge-
netics—it just says it's not enough." [16] Another individual, a
well-known physicist and author of a popular book on particle physics, said that he hadn't read Sheldrake's work in
any of its details but was still convinced that it was nonsense. And then for good measure he added, "Even if some
sort of anomalous statistical pattern is found in these tests,
it means nothing."

In spite of such hostility among some of his peers, Sheldrake's ideas seem to have touched some sort of collective
nerve in the general public, and vast numbers of people
continue to find the ramifications of his hypothesis ineluctably fascinating. In this regard, the London *Times* continues
to follow Sheldrake's work closely, and the BBC has produced a half dozen programs on his work. In the United
States, articles about Sheldrake's hypothesis have appeared
in *Science Digest, Esquire,* and the *Washington Post.* And on
recent visits he has addressed the physics department at the
University of California in Berkeley, the classes of leading
evolutionist Stephen Jay Gould at Harvard (Gould even allowed his students to participate in one of Sheldrake's experiments), SRI International in Menlo Park, the National
Institutes of Health, the U.S. Congressional Clearinghouse
on the Future, and the World Bank.

In the final examination, the most important aspect of
his hypothesis, says Sheldrake, is that it is testable. And if it
is found to be correct in its current form, Sheldrake stresses

FIGURE 11 *Solution to Sheldrake's puzzle pictures.*

that such experimental vindication might bring us closer to accepting M-fields as real entities. However, even if such evidence is found, Sheldrake does not believe that we will be able to observe M-fields directly. He suspects that M-fields—like gravitational and electromagnetic fields—will be found to be invisible, intangible, inaudible, tasteless, and odorless, and detectable only through their effects.

Intriguingly, if M-fields are discovered, Sheldrake believes that they may also shed new light on the mystery of consciousness itself. According to Sheldrake's hypothesis, M-fields manifest themselves primarily as deeply rooted habits. Since one of the most significant aspects of consciousness is its unique capacity to alter or change habit, Sheldrake suggests that perhaps consciousness functions as a mediator between the physical body and its M-fields. If this is the case, Sheldrake asserts that there would no longer be any reason to assume that our memories of past events are even stored materially in our brains. As he sees it, through a process similar to morphic resonance, what we perceive as memory may be the result of the brain tuning into its own past states. In other words, it is simply functioning as a tuning system rather than as a storage place for memories.

An argument against this is that states of consciousness are often associated with physiological activities within the body. Dreams, for instance, are invariably accompanied by rapid eye movements and by electrical rhythms of particular frequencies within the brain. To explain this apparent contradiction, Sheldrake offers the analogy of a car and its driver. Under certain conditions, when a car is driven its movements are closely connected with the actions of the driver. When the driver turns the steering wheel, the car turns, and so on. However, under other circumstances the connection between the car and driver is less distinct. For instance, when the car is in park and its engine is idling, the driver may be looking at a road map. In such a situation, although there is still a general relationship between the state of the car and what the driver is doing, there is no specific connection between the vibrations of the engine and the features of the map the driver is studying. Sheldrake suggests that similarly, the rhythmical electrical activity in the brain need bear no specific relationship to the images experienced in a dream.

If consciousness is little more than a driver inhabiting that three-pound lump of gray matter we know as our brain, the question remains—What is the substance of that driver? What is consciousness? The substance of consciousness may be unlike any substance with which we are currently familiar, and hence a new vocabulary might be needed before we can even begin to speak about it meaningfully. In the past several years a number of developments have occurred which shed some light on this question, and even point the way to such vocabulary. These developments, and the vocabulary they bring with them, are the subject of the next chapter.

# 4

# What and Where Is Consciousness?

In the past 15 years a philosophy of mind called
functionalism that is neither dualist nor materialist
has emerged from philosophical reflection on developments in artificial intelligence, computational
theory, linguistics, cybernetics and psychology. All
these fields, which are collectively known as the
cognitive sciences, have in common a certain level
of abstraction and a concern with systems that process information. Functionalism, which seeks to
provide a philosophical account of this level of abstraction, recognizes the possibility that systems as
diverse as human beings, calculating machines and
disembodied spirits could all have mental states.

— JERRY A. FODOR, *Scientific American*

WHEN I was an adolescent, one night I had an unusually
vivid dream. As it began I found myself hovering over my
body and looking down at myself asleep in the bed. The
experience was disconcerting, for everything about the
dream, my perceptions of myself still lying in the bed and
the familiar furnishings of my bedroom, seemed uncannily
real. Still, I remained convinced that it was all just a dream,
and set about to enjoy my newfound freedom.

I floated weightlessly out of my bedroom and into the
living room, still marveling at the fact that all of the features
of the house seemed identical to how I knew them in my
waking state. There was no spatial distortion of the size of
the rooms. All of the familiar objects and furnishings were

there. Nothing changed or flowed liquidly into something else, as things have a tendency to do in most normal dreams. Still, the sensation of flying was so blissful that I found it hard to concern myself about the strange condition I was in and just continued to drift on happily through the house.

Suddenly, as I swam like some airborne fish through the rooms, I found myself heading on a collision course with a large picture window. But before I had time to panic, I drifted through it, effortlessly, and looked back in astonishment to see that my passage had not affected it in the least. I continued on for a way, looking down at the dewy grass passing like the surface of some strange moon beneath me, and then suddenly nestled in the grass I saw a book.

I drifted close enough to read its title and saw that it was a collection of short stories by the nineteenth-century French author Guy de Maupassant. I was aware of who de Maupassant was, but he had no prominence in either my life or interests to make his appearance in my dreams explicable to me. I took this as proof positive that I was dreaming, because at last here was the absurdity in the landscape that one comes to expect in such nocturnal visions. Soon after I spotted the book, I drifted back into dreamlessness and didn't recall the incident until I woke up the following morning.

It was while I was on my way to school the next day that a neighbor stopped me. She told me that she had been walking in the woods near my house and that she thought she might have accidentally lost a library book during her excursion. She explained to me that it was a collection of short stories by Guy de Maupassant, and she asked me if I had seen it. Stunned, I related to her my experience of the night before, and together we strolled to the spot where I had seen the book in my dream. And there it was, nestled in the grass exactly as it had been when I had lazily floated over it.

My experience has several possible explanations. The

first is that my dream was simply a coincidence, or more accurately a remarkable series of coincidences.

A second explanation is that somehow the information about the lost book entered my consciousness subliminally, or without my knowing it. Numerous studies have shown that the human mind has a remarkable talent for absorbing information that we are not necessarily conscious of having absorbed. In this regard, I had not traveled to the area of the woods where the book had been lost between the time my neighbor lost it and the time I had the dream, so I could not have seen it in my peripheral vision and registered it unconsciously. I had also not seen my neighbor during this time, and so could not have known about it from some chance remark that she might have made and stored it away at an unconscious level. The only other possibility that I can conceive of is that perhaps some subtle clue was given in a previous conversation with my neighbor that allowed my unconscious mind to deduce that (1) she had a tendency to lose books and (2) the vagaries of her interests were leading her ultimately to the short stories of de Maupassant. But again, my conscious examination of my relationship and previous conversations with my neighbor, and my inexplicable knowledge of the book's location, make me feel that this is conceivable but implausible.

A third explanation is that my consciousness, or some subset of my self-awareness, left my body during its sleeping state and actually saw the book. My own prejudice is that the semantics, or wording, of this assessment may need refinement, but with the exception of the possible crudeness and approximation of such a remark, it is the likeliest of the three explanations. I base my conclusion not only on the impact my own experience had upon me, but also on the reading of the vast amount of literature suggestive of out-of-the-body experiences, or OBEs.

I have related my experience because it was the first time that a disconcerting and even scientifically outrageous idea occurred to me. My consciousness, and all of the sensations and percepts that I know as "me," were not as attached to my biological brain as I thought they were.

A similar "heresy" was recently proposed by a British neurologist named John Lorber when he addressed a 1980 conference of pediatricians and asked with a certain degree of seriousness, "Is the brain really necessary?" The strange sequence of events that caused Lorber to ask such a question actually began in the mid-1960s when he became aware of two children who each had a rather unusual problem.

Both were victims of hydrocephalus, or water on the brain, which is a condition characterized by an abnormal build-up of cerebrospinal fluid in the brain (hydrocephalics should not be confused with anencephalics, brainless individuals whose neural tube never closed properly). What was unusual about the children was that as a result of their hydrocephalus, neither showed any evidence of possessing a cerebral cortex (the part of the brain believed to be the seat of consciousness). However, in spite of this staggering impairment, the mental development of both children appeared to be normal. One of the children later died at the age of three months, but at twelve months the other was still healthy and normal mentally so far as could be judged, except that repeated medical experiments still provided no evidence of cerebral tissue. Lorber published an account of the incident in *Developmental Medicine and Child Neurology*, and like most profound anomalies that cannot be explained by the current scientific understanding, the account was neglected.[1]

Lorber's work progressed, however, and recently he encountered another incident that puts his previous discovery to shame. A colleague at Sheffield University came across a student with a slightly larger-than-normal head. The situation was not causing the student any problems, but because of Lorber's interest in such matters, the student was referred to him. Lorber ran a CAT scan (a type of noninvasive brain-scanning technique that determines different radio-densities in the brain) on the youth and discovered that although the boy had an IQ of 126, had gained a first-class honors degree in mathematics, and functioned in all other ways as completely normal, he had "virtually no brain." Lining his skull was only a thin layer of brain cells a millimeter or so thick, and the rest of his cranium was filled with cerebrospinal fluid.[2] Had his parents shone a flashlight through his head in a dark room when he had been a newborn infant and still possessed the delicate bones of a baby, the light would have shone through from one side to the other. The boy continues to live his life normally except for the fact that he is now aware that he possesses no brain.

There is also the story of the coroner as he related the cause of a young man's death to his parents. The man, it seems, had had gross hydrocephalus as an infant. However, the man had also had a "shunt" operation when he was a baby, a procedure in which a device known as a shunt is surgically implanted in the skull to drain off excess cerebrospinal fluid and thus save the child from brain damage and ultimate death. As far as the man and his parents knew, the shunt operation had been a success, for he had gone on to live a normal life and hold down an ordinary job.

All of this, however, was unknown to the coroner. He discovered that the man died when his shunt had ultimately broken down. He also discovered that the man, like Lorber's mathematics student, possessed only a minute rim of brain tissue. In relating all of this to the parents, he expressed his condolences, but then commented on the "relief" they must have felt at the fact that such a "vegetable" had finally ended his days. The dismayed parents explained to the coroner that the boy had been at work only two days before. And thereupon the embarrassed coroner no doubt apologized.[3]

Lorber has since gone on to discover numerous other individuals who function normally but possess no brain. For example, in an article published in *Science* in 1980, science writer Roger Lewin reported that at the Children's Hospital in Sheffield, Lorber has done more than 600 such scans on patients with hydrocephalus. In the study, he divided the patients into four groups: those with nearly normal brains, those with cerebrospinal fluid filling 50 to 70 percent of the cranium; those in which it fills 70 to 90 percent; and the most severe group, those in which cerebrospinal fluid fills 95 percent of the cranium. In this last group, which comprised just less than 10 percent of the study, half of the individuals were severely mentally disabled, but the remaining half possessed IQs greater than 100.[4]

Startling as it may seem, Lorber's discovery is nothing new. Patrick Wall, professor of anatomy at University College, London has observed, "Scores of similar accounts litter medical literature, and they go back a long way. But the important thing about Lorber is that he's done a long series of systematic scanning, rather than just dealing with anecdotes. He has gathered a remarkable set of data and he challenges, 'How do we explain it?' "[5]

Karl Lashley's discovery that memory is impaired but not obliterated by partial removal of various portions of the brain was astonishing enough. But the fact that under certain circumstances memory, and indeed all of the normal operations of consciousness, are not impaired when as much as 95 percent of the cranium is filled with nothing more than cerebrospinal fluid is nothing short of mind-boggling. What could possibly explain such a phenomenon?

Some, like Kenneth Till, a former neurosurgeon at the Great Ormond Street Hospital for Sick Children, London, refuse to believe that it is occurring at all, citing the difficulty of interpreting brain scans accurately as a possible explanation. Till believes that Lorber is being overdramatic when he says that someone has "virtually no brain." Lorber admits that interpreting brain scans can be tricky, but counters, "Of course these results are dramatic, but they're not overdramatic. One would not make the claim if one did not have the evidence." To the argument that he has not precisely quantified the amount of brain tissue missing, he adds, "I can't say whether the mathematics student has a brain weighing 50 grams or 150 grams, but it's clear that it is nowhere near the normal 1.5 kilograms."[6]

When confronted with Lorber's findings, most neurologists assume that the only possible explanation is that there is a great deal of redundancy in the brain and that the deeper structures of the brain somehow take over the duties of the missing cortex. Some, however, feel that this is merely a way of avoiding the profound puzzle that Lorber has uncovered. For example, Wall states, "To talk of redundancy in the brain is an intellectual cop-out to try to get round something you don't understand." Norman Geschwind, a neurologist at Boston's Beth Israel Hospital, agrees: "Certainly the brain has a remarkable capacity for reassigning functions following trauma, but you can usually pick up some kind of deficit with the right tests, even after apparently full recovery."[7]

What, then, is the explanation? Currently, the consensus is that no one really knows. About the only thing that is admitted by those who are willing to consider Lorber's work honestly is that the long cherished notion that the cortex is the sole seat of consciousness in the human body has now been gravely cast in doubt. Most neurologists remain convinced that consciousness is a consequence of the anatomy and physiology of the cerebral cortex, and though a great deal is known about the biological workings of the brain, when backed into a corner, most scientists are forced to admit that no one really has any idea how the brain contrives to produce consciousness.

What and where is consciousness? This question caused great thinkers of the past such as Descartes to propose that although consciousness and the brain are clearly related, there remains an essential difference between the two. As

Descartes saw it, mind and all things mental constitute a world apart from physical matter and work according to their own system of dynamic laws. In the cognitive sciences such a belief is known as *dualism*.

With the tremendous flowering of the mechanistic approach, or the belief that anything can be understood if one divides it up into enough tiny components, dualism eventually fell out of scientific favor. Given that it is quite easy to search for and discover physical causes for most of the events that we see in the world around us, the idea that a nonphysical entity, consciousness, could somehow intrude upon the world of matter and control and influence a physical entity such as the brain, came to be regarded by many scientists as unacceptably metaphysical. The late Oxford philosopher Gilbert Ryle derisively called a proposed nonphysical consciousness the "horse in the locomotive" or the "ghost in the machine." This belief, that dualism should be abandoned and the only thing that should be studied are the physical components of the brain, is known in the cognitive sciences as *materialism*.

Although materialism reached the height of its popularity with the work of such radical behaviorists as B. F. Skinner, who developed an elaborate world view completely denying any connection between behavior and mental causes, it is still embraced by many scientists today. For example, in his bestseller *The Dragons of Eden*, Carl Sagan purports to write an entire book on the nature and evolution of human intelligence, but contains no entries in his index for such words as *consciousness*, *mind*, or *awareness*, and favors instead such entries as *synapse*, *thalamus*, *neuron*, and *cerebellum*.

In the past several decades, however, materialism has come under increasing fire by many scientists. Radical behaviorists had predicted that as psychology developed it would understand human behavior more and more in terms of stimuli and responses, and less and less in terms of mental causes. However, this has not happened. On the contrary, psychologists point out that as their field has continued to mature, the panorama of mental states that must be invoked to account for experimental observations has only grown more elaborate.

And perhaps the most succinct condemnation of materialism has come from an unlikely quarter. It is that pinnacle of mechanist achievement, the computer, which has caused many scientists to start thinking again about the ineffable mysteries of consciousness. Specifically, this thinking has come from the expanding new field of "artificial intelligence" (known to its aficionados as *AI*). In the past decade or so the attempt to create a computer actually capable of thought has yielded some rather startling conclusions about the nature of consciousness and a possible alternative definition to both dualism and materialism.

## CONSCIOUSNESS AS SOFTWARE

In its current state, the field of AI is certainly unique among all the various branches of science. Although many physicists do not like to admit so in print, in private conversation they reveal their discomfort with the philosophical ponderings that often sprout up around their work. The reason often given for this feeling is that experimentation, not philosophy, is what moves science ahead. I suspect also that such physicists are so deeply trained to deal only with tangibles that they simply want to get on with the "game" of science. Similarly, Tufts University philosopher Daniel C. Dennett states, "Many psychologists and brain scientists are embarrassed by the philosophical questions, and wish no one would ask them. . . ."[8]

In struggling to arrive at a way of creating artificial intelligence, however, many computer scientists gradually have reached the conclusion that to build a machine capable of something resembling human thought, one must also arrive at a coherent point of view or philosophy of mind. Thus, unlike most scientific disciplines, AI research actively encourages the contributions of philosophers and has become a strange amalgam of the work of engineers and speculative thinkers, of mathematicians, linguists, and even psychologists. It is out of this diverse synthesis of thinkers that a possible new way of understanding the phenomenon of consciousness has arisen.

The best way to begin to visualize this new understanding of consciousness is to employ a little bit of backward thinking. While most AI researchers take it as a given that we will ultimately develop a computer capable of simulating human thought, not all scientists and philosophers agree. For the skeptical it is perhaps more palatable to believe that intelligent life could exist elsewhere in the universe, and that extraterrestrial life need not necessarily be based on the carbon molecule, as is all Earth life. Perhaps somewhere in the universe there exists intelligent life whose biology is based on silicon. Or perhaps in some interstellar dust cloud there exists intelligent life composed solely of radiation. If we seriously entertain any one of these propositions, we also must admit that what we know as consciousness is no longer synonymous with possessing a brain as we know it. Does this mean that materialism is wrong and dualism should be accepted? Most AI researchers feel dualism is tantamount to believing in ghosts. To find a way out of the dilemma they have formulated a third possibility.

Perhaps consciousness is not a substance but is *structure*. In other words, perhaps to be an intelligent and thinking being does not depend so much on what one's parts are but on the way that those parts are put together. The conscious self stands in the same relationship to the physical brain as a mathematical equation stands to a physical computer. Put another way, the consciousness is the "software" or program that allows the "hardware" of the computer to operate or function. Hence, this new way of looking at consciousness is called *functionalism*.

To better visualize what is meant by the idea of consciousness as software, a lesson can be drawn from an early experiment in robotics performed in the 1940s by neurologist Grey Walter of the Burden Neurological Institute in Bristol, England. Walter set about to build two robot tortoises. To construct his mechanical creatures, Walter gave each one of them three wheels (the front one for steering), a revolving photoelectric cell (as a rudimentary sense of sight) and an electric contact on the front of each of their plastic shells (as a rudimentary sense of touch).

In addition, Walter provided each of his mechanical tortoises with a battery and a motor, and connected all of these components together in a manner that would allow the tortoises to interact with their environment. Each of the tortoises was "light hungry" and would roll around looking for food in the form of a brightly lit "hutch." Walter also programmed his tortoises to be "electricity hungry," and to this end the hutch also contained electrical contacts that enabled the robots to recharge their batteries. However, their electricity hunger was designed to come into play only when the voltage in their storage batteries fell below 5.5 volts, and was designed to shut off and allow the tortoises to feel "satiated" when it reached a level of 7 volts.

With these simple components and constraints, Walter reports that once they were set into motion, his robots, whom he called Elmer and Elsie, behaved in a remarkably lifelike manner. For example, after they had reached the 7 volt mark in their hutch, Elmer and Elsie would retire in stillness to "digest" their meal of electrical current. After the voltage in their storage batteries once again fell below this threshold they would "play," or wander around in search of a comfortable spot of light to sit in until their hunger threshold was reached and they were forced to search for their hutch once again.

Walter was surprised to find that this simple feedback loop between his tortoises' needs and their environment also resulted in a wide variety of unexpected behavior, from displays of primitive forms of discernment and memory, to the setting of priorities in overcoming obstacles, fits of frustration, and even a semblance of self-recognition. Most amazing of all, Walter reports that in spite of the fact that his robots were almost identical in design, they even developed different personalities. As he rolled through his electrical life, Elmer showed a marked inclination toward moodiness, hiding under furniture for long periods of time and only coming out when he was hungry. Elsie, on the other hand, was far more adventurous and moved around more, but this fact, Walter says, also made her behave far more "impatiently" when confronting obstacles than her shy and docile brother.[9]

According to the functionalist approach, such differences in personality are not due to Elmer and Elsie possessing different "ghosts" in their machine. Nor would the reasons for their existence be evident if one dismantled Elmer and Elsie and carefully scrutinized their parts. Instead, Elmer and Elsie's different personalities manifest only after those parts have been put together in a very special way, and the differences between them is, in turn, due to minute differences in design. In other words, the thing that makes Elmer and Elsie behave as different and unique personalities does not exist as a "substance" or an "energy." It exists only in the realm of pure information, and as such, is in the same class of things as the software or intangible mathematical program that allows the hardware of a computer to run.

At first glance it may seem that functionalism is little different from materialism, but this is not the case. Unlike the materialist, the functionalist does not foresee, even in principle, that the phenomenon of consciousness will ever be understood by reducing a thinking entity to its constituent parts. Rather, functionalism proposes that a thinking entity is, indeed, more than the sum of its parts, and that consciousness is an emergent property that manifests when a certain level of organization is reached among such interacting parts—be those parts neurons or silicon chips.

Following this, functionalism proposes that mentalistic concepts should not be eliminated from science and that consciousness should be considered an actual phenomenon worthy of study. As Dennett, himself a functionalist, puts it:

We must not suppose that science teaches us that every *thing* anyone would ever want to take seriously is identifiable as a collection of particles moving about in space and time. Some people may think it is just common sense (or just good scientific thinking) to suppose *you* are nothing but a particular living, physical organism—a moving mound of atoms—but in fact this idea exhibits a lack of scientific imagination, not hard-headed sophistication. One doesn't have to believe in *ghosts* to believe in *selves* that have an identity that transcends any particular living body.[10]

Once again, as with Bohm's implicate order and Pribram's holographic model of human memory, we have an example of a phenomenon that cannot be understood by reducing it to smaller units. Such an approach, the belief that some phenomena can only be understood in terms of integrated wholes, is known as "holism." At this point it might be worthwhile to make a comment on the entire issue of holism versus mechanism, or reductionism. Many scientists prickle at any talk about the benefits of a holistic approach. Often it is because they equate any suggestion of holism with the complete overthrow of the mechanistic/reductionist creed, but in the case of functionalism, at least, this is simply not the case. In his essay "Ant Fugue" in *Godel, Escher, Bach,* computer scientist and functionalist Douglas Hofstadter offers a good way of accommodating both points of view. Each provides a different level of description, and each is therefore useful for separate purposes. A holistic approach may help us gain a better grasp of ecological interconnections, but it won't help us determine the chemical composition of a polluted lake; similarly, reductionism may help us unravel the neurophysiology of brain processes, but will never explain why different people respond differently to the same painting.

We now come to the question suggested by the dream experience I related at the beginning of this chapter. That is, if functionalism is correct about the *what* of consciousness—that it is pure information or structure—what about the *where* of consciousness? Is it possible for "software" to move through space?

Some functionalists place consciousness in the same spatiotemporal state as "information" and thus do not believe that it is meaningful to speak of it as existing apart from some sort of hardware or other material context. "Where in time and space does "The Star Spangled Banner" exist?" asks Dennett.[11] Others come close to suggesting that perhaps the software of consciousness can "move" about on its own. For example, in a recent article in *Scientific American*, M.I.T. psychologist and philosopher Jerry A. Fodor asserts that functionalism recognizes the possibility that disembodied spirits can have mental states, but he does not elaborate any further on this remarkable proposition.[12] Similarly, in a recent interview, computer expert Donald MacKay of the University of Keele, England, also admitted the possibility of the "human equation" surviving the death of its host's brain but added no thoughts on how such survival might be possible.[13]

Information from another branch of science offers further intriguing evidence of this possibility. In a 1982 study, psychiatrist Fowler Jones of the University of Kansas asked 420 randomly selected people whether they had ever had an out-of-body experience, and 339 replied that they had. What are such experiences? Jones says, "All we can say at this point is that people who have such experiences feel they're quite real. They describe them in various ways, but the common denominator is that the mind, the "I" part of the personality, the thinking-feeling part, is no longer located inside the physical body but is deposited somewhere else in the environment. It is as if they have a mobile center of consciousness located just a few feet, or several miles, from the physical body."[14]

Jones emphasizes that OBEs are experienced by normal, healthy, and intelligent people. He also does not believe that they are merely dreams. If they were, he adds, it would be impossible to explain why so many events witnessed during an OBE turn out to be real. In his study, Jones interviewed one man whose mind left his body and traveled to a location where several people were plotting his murder. After returning to his body, the man confronted one of the conspirators and frightened her into admitting their plan.[15]

After his death it was revealed that Barney Clark, the world's first artificial-heart recipient, had several OBEs during the course of his medical ordeal. According to his widow, on several occasions after he regained consciousness following surgery, Clark described having observed the entire operation from a point outside his body and was able to give accurate details of events that transpired while he was under anesthesia.

Clark's experience is not unique. OBEs are frequently reported by people during surgery and other severe physical trauma resulting in unconsciousness. In a typical experience the individual suddenly finds himself floating in a disembodied state above his own body and watching as doctors or friends try to revive the inanimate physical form below. Although such experiences are usually viewed by the medical profession as products of the imagination, the evidence is mounting that some further explanation must be offered.

For example, Dr. Michael B. Sabom, a cardiologist and Professor of Medicine at Emory University and a staff physician at the Atlanta VA Medical Center, counted himself among the skeptics until he began to take a serious look at the phenomenon. In one study, Sabom formed a control group of 25 "seasoned cardiac patients" who had been hospitalized for heart attacks but had never experienced an OBE, and asked them to describe the medical procedure that had taken place during their resuscitation. Of these, 20 made a major error in their descriptions of what transpired; three gave correct but very general descriptions, and two had no ideas at all about what had taken place.

Sabom then amassed a group of 32 patients who had reported OBEs during their heart attacks and asked them to describe the details of their resuscitation. Of these, 26 gave correct but very general descriptions; six gave specific and verifiable details of their own particular resuscitation, and one man gave an account that was "extremely accurate in portraying the appearance, technique, and sequence of the CPR (cardiopulmonary resuscitation)."[16] Sabom states:

Following our interview, I came to know this man quite well and visited him several times at his home. At no time did I find any indication that he possessed more than a layman's knowledge of medicine. Moreover, from the flow of our initial conversation during the interview itself (which was unplanned and unrehearsed), it is evident that many of the details he recalled were given in response to my own probings and were not volunteered, as might have been expected from an informed individual attempting to "reconstruct" the events of the resuscitation from a detailed knowledge of the procedure. I was also struck by his reaction to my inadvertent use of the word "paddle" to describe the instrument that is held on the patient's chest during electrical defibrillation. "Paddle" is a widely used term for these instruments and is so ingrained in my mind that I use it without thinking. The man demonstrated his unfamiliarity with this word, however, by his response: "They weren't paddles, Doctor. They were round disks with a handle on them. No paddles."[17]

Some researchers have tried to explain such experiences by suggesting that the subjects were semiconscious and therefore able to recall what transpired, but Sabom notes that while occasional patients remain semiconscious during surgery, there is substantial evidence to refute this explanation. Memories of surgical procedures by semiconscious patients tend to be of conversations between doctors and nurses as opposed to being visual. They also tend to be disjointed and dreamlike as opposed to the highly lucid descriptions offered by near-death patients experiencing OBEs. Lastly, such memories are frequently unpleasant and wrought by an awareness of pain, whereas OBEs by near-death patients are invariably described as extremely pleasant and totally devoid of pain.

Another possibility that has been offered is that near-death OBEs are the product of a particular belief system or religious persuasion, but Sabom also does not find any evidence to support this conclusion. In a study designed to address this issue he found that 42 percent of randomly interviewed near-death survivors experienced OBEs but revealed no correlation to religious background or prior knowledge of OBEs. Indeed, Sabom found that OBEs occurred in a completely random cross section of near-death survivors regardless of their "age, sex, race, area of residence, size of home community, education, occupation, religion, frequency of church attendance, and previous knowledge of NDE (near-death experiences)."[18]

What is happening during such experiences? In his 1982 book, *Recollections of Death,* Sabom concludes, "If the human brain is actually composed of two fundamental elements—the 'mind' and the 'brain'—then could the near-death crisis even somehow trigger a transient splitting of the mind from the brain in many individuals? . . . My own beliefs on this matter are leaning in this direction. The out-of-body hypothesis simply seems to fit best with the data at hand."[19]

As I stated earlier, I also believe that something tantamount to the consciousness leaving the body does occur during an OBE, although "leaving the body" may not be the best choice of words for summing up the process. In his 1984 book, *Star Wave: Mind, Consciousness, and Quantum Physics,* physicist Fred Alan Wolf predicts that the "mind will not be found in any physical pattern of our brain material."[20] Wolf believes that the ultimate stuff of consciousness lies in the ghostly and incorporeal world of the quantum itself. Given that there is now persuasive evidence that this world is nonlocal, it may be that consciousness, like the quantum, does not possess any single and precise location at all. Sometimes it seems to be inside our heads. Sometimes, via the infinite interconnectedness of the quantum landscape, it seems to be hovering over a lost copy of a book of de Maupassant short stories. But in truth it never "goes" anywhere at all. It simply accesses whatever perspective on the universe it wants via the nonlocal realm from which it operates.

Another question that arises from the functionalist approach is, How could something that exists purely as information bring about mental causes? It seems somewhat apparent that the stream of symbols that comprise our thoughts can initiate physical activity. For example, when we think of sitting down in a chair, the body obliges us, and we sit down in a chair. If our thought of sitting down in the chair exists only as information and is therefore immaterial, how does this immaterial something reach across the rift between the symbolic and the actual to spur the body into activity?

This is an important question and one that forms the crux of the mind-body problem. To date, no one has provided an adequate answer, and even functionalism fails to provide a satisfactory solution. To understand the relationship between the software of the mind and the hardware of the neurons the mind seems to be controlling, Hofstadter invokes the analogy of a computer constructed out of dominoes. Modern computers have microelectric circuits that are activated by electricity, but early computers had actual moving parts—interconnected series of relays and switches arranged in a manner that enabled them to perform mathematical calculations. Although these early computers are now primitive by today's standards, they had the advantage of allowing one to actually watch the physical processes taking place inside them when they were calculating the solution to a problem.

Hofstadter suggests that it is possible to imagine an even simpler computer composed of intricately interconnected series of domino chains. In such a computer each domino would be equipped with a little time-delayed spring underneath it so that it could fall and stand back up as many times as might be required. Properly arranged, such an arrangement of domino chains could be made to perform mathematical calculations in the same manner as early computers. As Hofstadter points out, the various pathways and branching loops of such a domino chain computer could be viewed as crudely analogous to the interconnected networks of neurons in the human brain.

Hofstadter now asks us to imagine arranging the chains of dominoes in a way that will program the computer to break the number 641 into the product of its prime factors. After this is done one could then topple the first domino and sit and watch as various sequences of dominoes collapse and straighten again as the computer struggles to solve the problem. During this entire process one might decide to watch one particular domino and ask, Why doesn't this particular domino ever fall down? An answer on one level would be, because its predecessor never falls down. In Hofstadter's terminology this is a low-level explanation. As he points out, what one really wants—the only satisfying answer—is an answer on the conceptual level of the program. That answer is, it never falls down because it is in a stretch of dominoes that gets activated only when a divisor is found. However, 641 has no divisors—it is prime. So the reason the domino never falls down has nothing to do with physics or domino chains. Its cause exists purely in the realm of information, in the fact that 641 is prime.

Does this mean that higher-level laws such as those contained in computer programs somehow govern the system above and beyond lower-level laws? The answer that Hofstadter gives to this question is an emphatic *no*. As he states, "We do not believe that there is some as-yet-undiscovered 'mental magnetism' through which concepts could 'reach down' and, by some sort of 'semantic potential,' alter the paths of particles, making them deviate from what present-day physics would predict."[21]

Counter to this, one might ask, Then what *caused* the entire calculation to initiate in the first place? Hofstadter's response is that we can only ask the question if we understand that we are really dealing with two levels of description. One is the reductionist level that governs the causal chains connecting all the dominoes. The other is the holistic level that governs the mysterious operations that take place in the software realm of thought. Thus, Hofstadter concedes that wholes such as the software of consciousness "do indeed exert a visible effect on their parts, do indeed possess 'downward causality,' " but he alleges to avoid that old bugaboo of dualism—how the immaterial can exert a physical influence over the material—by saying that this downward causality is not the same as the causality spoken of in classical physics. It is, in fact, an illusion brought about because of the necessity to translate between the two modes of description.[22]

For Hofstadter the fact that one level of description seems to be required to describe the mind and another level of description is required to describe the biochemical workings of the brain is explanation enough for the apparent interaction that occurs between the two. Consequently, Hofstadter's brand of functionalism is similar to materialism in that it predicts that a totally reductionist explanation of the brain is possible. It simply predicts that such an explanation would also be incomprehensible unless one included with it a second and more holistic mode of description.

Hofstadter's explanation is clever, but I believe it is ultimately a semantic obfuscation. Although the toppling of any given domino in our computer may be contingent on whether 641 is prime or not, even Hofstadter's analogy requires that something "push" the first domino in the sequence to get the entire process started. Hofstadter's way of viewing things still does not explain how a thought initiates a change in the physical world. It does not explain what "pushes" the various neurons in the brain to get them going in the first place.

It is not surprising that Hofstadter goes to such lengths to avoid suggesting that any unknown forces are responsible for this pushing. The current and pervasive influence of the Edge of the Map Syndrome has made it very unfashionable for theoreticians to suggest that there are any energies or influences outside of the present scientific understanding.

Not all researchers are victims of fashion. British neurophysiologist Sir John Eccles, who won a Nobel Prize in 1963 for his pioneering research on the synapse, braves the scorn of his colleagues and still calls himself a dualist. Eccles believes that consciousness is a nonmaterial something that does indeed exist apart from our biological selves and causally determines which of our neurons fire and which do not. Moreover, because of current advances in our knowledge of neurophysiology, Eccles recently announced that he can even specify in which precise location in the brain this interaction between matter and spirit takes place.

## BIOCHEMICAL EVIDENCE FOR THE EXISTENCE OF THE HUMAN SOUL

The region of the brain about which Eccles makes this remarkable assertion is known as the *supplementary motor area,* or SMA, and it is located at the very top of the brain (see Figure 12). The SMA was first discovered in the 1920s by the late Canadian neurophysiologist Wilder Penfield in the

SUPPLEMENTARY MOTOR AREA

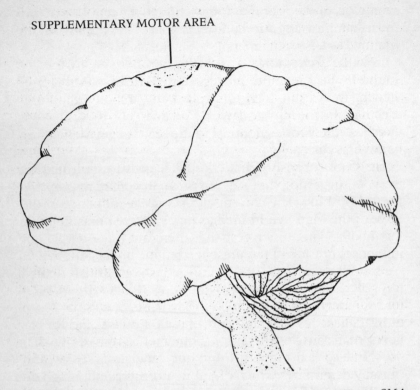

FIGURE 12    *The location of the* supplementary motor area *or SMA in the human brain. Neurophysiologist Sir John Eccles proposes that this is the site of interaction between mind and body.*

course of his famous search for the area of the brain responsible for epilepsy, but his discovery was neglected for decades. Slowly, however, researchers became more interested in its functions. Neurophysiologists Robert Porter and Cobie Brinkman surgically implanted microelectrodes in the SMA of a monkey and discovered that about one-tenth of a second *before* the monkey pulled a lever to obtain a food reward, the cells in its SMA began to fire. What was significant about this was that Porter and Brinkman discovered that the monkey's SMA began to discharge well before the cells in its motor cortex (the portion of the brain concerned with muscular movement) or indeed in any other part of the brain were activated.[23]

The next important discovery regarding the SMA came in the 1960s when neurophysiologists Hans Kornhuber and Luder Deecke developed a method for measuring minute electrical potentials occurring in various regions of a patient's scalp. Kornhuber and Deecke discovered what is now known as the *readiness potential,* or the fact that almost one second before carrying out a simple voluntary movement—such as the bending of a finger—the human brain displays a gradual increase in negative electrical potential. This increase is the brain's way of getting ready to make a voluntary movement, and Kornhuber and Deecke discovered that it was greatest in the SMA. However, they discovered that it was also large over the rest of the motor cortex, which caused many neurophysiologists to conclude that the act of mental intention (the mind's decision to move) was not localized, but widely dispersed over the brain.[24]

In 1980, a research group headed by neurophysiologists Nils Lassen and Per Roland of the University of Lund in Sweden published new evidence about the SMA that challenges the view that mental intention is widely dispersed over the brain. Lassen and Roland used new techniques developed to enable researchers to look more closely than ever before at the operations of the living brain. It is this new evidence that Eccles believes provides biochemical evidence of the interaction between the brain and a nonphysical consciousness.

The new techniques are based on several very simple premises. First, it is known that the blood flow to different parts of the nervous system is very delicately controlled by the vascular system. It is also known that brain activity consumes energy and oxygen just as muscle activity does. The Swedish group thus realized that if they developed a way of mapping the flow of blood as it courses through the brain, they would have a way of "seeing" which parts of the brain were busiest during various prescribed operations.[25]

To accomplish this task, Lassen and Roland and their colleagues injected a trace amount of a radioactive substance into a patient's bloodstream, and then, with a battery of 254 radiation detectors assembled in a helmet over the scalp, they measured the areas where the radiation, and hence the blood flow, was most concentrated.

During one of the tests of this procedure they then asked a patient to perform what the group referred to as the motor sequence test, a procedure in which the thumb has to touch in quick succession finger *1* twice, finger *2* once, finger *3* three times, and finger *4* twice. With only a minimal pause the patient was asked to perform the original sequence in reverse order, then in the original order, then in the reverse order, and so forth throughout the duration of the test. The patient was allowed to practice the sequences before the test began, but the sequences chosen were purposefully difficult so that the movements required continuous conscious attention and never became automatic.

What Lassen and Roland found initially were findings similar to those obtained by Kornhuber and Deecke, that a fraction of a second before movement is initiated there are significant increases in the blood flow to both the SMA and the motor areas of the brain. It was while performing a variation of the motor sequence test that they obtained their remarkable and controversial results. In a variation of the experiment called the "internal programming test," the patient was asked to carry out the same difficult sequences, only *mentally* and with no accompanying physical movement whatsoever. As expected, when patients performed this procedure, there was no increase in blood flow to the motor areas of their brains. However, Lassen and Roland discovered that the SMA region was still activated almost as much as when such movements were actually performed. Moreover, it was discovered that when the patient was asked to perform a simple movement and repeat it until it became habitual and could occur without conscious attention, the anticipatory activity in the SMA also disappeared.[26]

Eccles concluded, "It is important to recognize that this burst of discharge of the observed SMA cell was not triggered by some other nerve cell of the SMA or elsewhere in the brain. . . . So we have here an irrefutable demonstration that a mental act of intention *initiates* the burst of discharges of a nerve cell."[27]

In his 1984 book, *The Wonder of Being Human*, coauthored with Georgetown University psychologist Daniel N. Robinson, Eccles cites other recent discoveries concerning the SMA. For example, when patients who have Parkinson's disease—and hence have a great deal of difficulty in initiating voluntary movement—are tested in this fashion, it has been discovered that as they attempt to move, there is very little activity in their motor cortex. However, the neurons in their SMA region continue to fire normally. States Eccles, "It can be concluded that this evidence again demonstrates the priority of the SMA in the initiation of a voluntary act."[28]

If this is not enough, Eccles points out that it has been found that different acts of mental intention initiate different patterns of neural discharge in the SMA. Eccles concludes that some sort of complex code is involved and that the nonphysical mind is actually "playing" the 50 million or so neurons in the SMA region as if they were the keys to some sort of piano. How does one's mind learn the vast repertoire of coded sequences involved in operating this body of ours? Eccles believes that this is the learned process of a lifetime, from infancy onward. Where might such a nonphysical mind arise from? Eccles suggests that it "entered" our physical brain sometime during embryological development, and thus it is conceivable to him that such a nonphysical self might also survive the death of the material body.[29]

As might be expected, many brain researchers do not

agree with Eccles' conclusions. Both the materialist and the functionalist points of view hold that all neural firings in the brain have physical causes. Thus, there can be no neural activity like that found in the SMA region without there being activity in some other region of the brain. And if one asks what causes the activity in this other region, both the materialist and the functionalist answer that it is activity in yet another region of the brain, and so on, in a kind of vicious cycle.

Nonetheless, accepting the existence of such a conundrum is preferable to most researchers than believing, as Eccles does, that something ghostly is playing the keyboard in the SMA region. As Princeton psychologist George A. Miller states, "Most scientists are materialists, confident that all physical effects have physical causes. That the cause of activity in SMA cells is not presently known will not persuade them that the cause must be mental."[30]

Although functionalism still leaves many questions unanswered, it has at least allowed discussions of consciousness as a phenomenon to once again become acceptable in scientific circles. The radical behaviorist's belief that all references to consciousness should be banished from scientific thinking has always carried an air of paradox about it (imagine sitting around and being conscious of the fact that there is no such thing as consciousness). Small though this functionalist contribution may seem, its importance should not be underestimated.

Another important advance that functionalism has effected in our understanding of consciousness is its suggestion that consciousness behaves in many ways that are characteristic of the way we expect information to behave. By recognizing the informationlike aspects of consciousness, functionalism has succeeded in doing what neither materialism nor dualism was able to do. It has opened the door on a possible avenue for further understanding the nature of consciousness.

The only question that remains is whether the pure information, or software of consciousness, is merely an abstraction, a metaphorical way of thinking about consciousness, as Hofstadter believes. Or is it an actuality that can indeed interact with the physical universe, as Eccles believes? Put another way, is the software of consciousness a "nothing" or is it a "something?" My own feeling is that phenomena such as out-of-the-body experiences and the sudden and inexplicable neural activity in the SMA region following mental intention indicate that the software of consciousness is most definitely a "something." However, the fact that our best scientific efforts have not yet been able to detect what this something is indicates that it is quite unlike the matter and energy of our classical understanding.

By what process might something that is not yet measurable exert an effect on our physical world? The answer to this question is not known, but it does not present an insurmountable stumbling block. For example, we do not yet know what process allows the two photons in the double-slit experiment to interact, and yet the Aspect experiment has shown that such an interaction does take place. Perhaps the software of consciousness exerts an influence on the neurons in the SMA region of our brains via a similar quantum process.

We also do not know what mysterious alchemy enables the human consciousness to interact and help create what it observes as the quantum world. Again this process does not involve any transfer of matter or energy as we currently understand the terms. Perhaps the interaction between the software of consciousness and the physical brain belongs to the same family of processes as this currently unfathomable transaction.

Whatever the case, what is intriguing and perhaps profoundly significant about the mind-body problem is that it has brought us to the same strange precipice that has been arrived at in quantum physics. We have reached the edge of physical reality as we know it, and still something seems to lie beyond, something that we cannot yet weigh or measure and still seems to have a profound effect on the physical world.

What is this something? I believe that, despite its flaws, functionalism comes close to being correct in calling it pure information. However, far from being nothing, I believe that various branches of science such as functionalism and quantum physics are leading us to a new Platonism. Just as Plato believed that ideas are real and possess an independent existence above and beyond the world of objects, I believe that science is in the first stages of accepting that—far from being merely descriptive—such hitherto second-class entities as "thought," "software," and "pure information" are real and even more fundamental than the world of matter.

We will return to this notion in later chapters, but for the moment let us put aside the question of whether the software of consciousness is a "something" or a "nothing," and proceed only with the assumption that it is a "nothing," simply a descriptive way of viewing certain organizations of matter. As we will see in the next chapter, even this idea alone has some profound and startling ramifications.

# 5

# A Dance of Interacting Parts

> The right way to begin to think about the pattern which connects is to think of it as *primarily* (whatever that means) a dance of interacting parts and only secondarily pegged down by various sorts of physical limits. . . .
>
> — GREGORY BATESON, *Mind and Nature*

ONE of the major qualms critics of functionalism have is its assertion that mentality need not always be a biological phenomenon. As philosopher John Searles summarized in a 1983 symposium on the computer sponsored by The New York Academy of Sciences, "They're saying the brain doesn't matter . . . that any system whatever, whether it's beer cans, or . . . stones laid on . . . squares, any system at all will have to have mental states in exactly the same sense that you and I do because all there is to having mental states is instantiating the right program."[1] Searles, a staunch critic of functionalism, finds such a view "preposterous." His objections notwithstanding, this conclusion remained the working premise of numerous other leading proponents of AI in the symposium.

The most startling proposal of functionalism is that the parts constituting a mental system don't matter. One question that quickly follows is, What criteria might we use to recognize that a system composed of parts radically different from neurons is also functioning as a mind? Some research-

ers believe that the answer to this question leads to a remarkable reassessment of living processes in general.

Although his name was not mentioned at the conference, one such researcher was the late anthropologist, Gregory Bateson. Throughout his life, Bateson—who was the
son of geneticist William Bateson and was once married to
Margaret Mead—devoted a good deal of his time to the
formulation of just such a criterion of mind. In his 1980
book *Mind and Nature*, his last work published before his
death, he offered his conclusions.

Although Bateson did not mention the term functionalism in any of his writings, his point of view was often identical to that put forward by the functionalists. For example,
like the functionalists he believed that mind was an explanatory principle necessary to the understanding of human
behavior. And like the functionalists he was dissatisfied with
both materialism and dualism, and chose the middle ground
that mind should be regarded as pure information. He
stated, "Mind is empty; it is nothing. It exists only in its
ideas, and these again are nothings." [2]

What divided Bateson from the functionalists is that he
recognized the "no-thing" nature of mind almost half a century ago and proceeded to spend a good deal of his professional career trying to understand how "something" that
seems to be "no-thing" can produce such diverse phenomena as our sense of self, the ability to learn and assimilate
new information, our wisdom and folly, and the entire panorama of human behavior.

The answer Bateson arrived at is that this "no-thing"
possesses quite a complex dynamic, and in spite of the fact
that it is neither a substance nor an energy, it seems to flow
in complex rivulets within minds and between minds, interpenetrating all that we know as human in patterns that
possess a mysterious regularity. It is the regularities of these
patterns, Bateson proposed, that provide us with the best
criteria for defining mind.

One regularity Bateson noted in the dynamics of the human mind is that the information involved in mental processes flows in circular and/or more complex chains of determination, not only within the brain but between the brain and the environment. Thus, if we discover a "something" that is pumping information out like a beacon, no matter how clever the information may seem, there is no reason to suspect that it is functioning as a mind unless it also seems capable of taking information in and incorporating it in some way with the information it is giving out.

A second important criterion of mind that Bateson set forth is that the something often uses this circular flow of information to self-regulate and maintain its own identity. For example, if the something receives the information—perhaps in the form of extreme heat—that it is in danger, it will not remain passive but will react in some way. Different somethings will, of course, react differently to different types of information, but all things that we should define as minds will utilize at least some of the circular flow of information passing through them to self-maintain.

It is obvious that the human mind fulfills both of Bateson's criteria. However, what also becomes obvious after a little thought is that nonliving systems such as Walter's robot tortoises, mentioned in the preceding chapter, also fulfill both of these criteria of mind. Both robots processed circular flows of information, and both utilized the circuit of information to self-regulate, as, for instance, when they had "eaten" enough electricity and pulled away from the electrical contacts in their hutch.

That human minds and certain nonliving systems operate similarly is, of course, the central thesis of the science of *cybernetics*—the study of self-regulating systems, both mechanical and biological—founded in the 1940s by M.I.T. mathematician Norbert Weiner. Weiner's science helped coalesce Bateson's thinking on the matter. However, it was Bateson's genius to expand the concept further and see the same criteria of mind at work in a host of other unexpected phenomena.

For example, while studying the Iatmul tribe on the Sepik River in New Guinea, Bateson discerned that the flow of information in the cultural dynamics of the tribe also followed the same cybernetic principles that he was struggling to arrive at in his criteria of mind. From this Bateson realized that virtually all social organizations, from the so-called primitive to the modern, are organized according to cybernetic principles. Like Walter's robot tortoises, communities of people take information in and give it out in circular patterns. Similarly, although certain social forces such as the advent of a new industry may work to tear the community apart, built into the values of virtually all human cultures are customs, rituals, and belief systems that function as fail-safe mechanisms to enable the communities to struggle to self-regulate and preserve themselves.

Bateson perceived that the same cybernetic principles were at work in the natural world as well. A rain forest employs complex circular chains of energy and information to self-regulate and maintain itself. Similarly, pollutants such as DDT also follow cybernetic principles in the way they circulate throughout the world's ecosystem.[3] In short, Bateson began to perceive that his criteria of mind were at work in virtually all of the biological workings on the planet, from the way alcoholics rationalize their addiction to themselves to the apparent communication that takes place between dolphins, from the way that schizophrenia develops to the way a seashell forms.

Most importantly, Bateson saw that the process of evolution, the way that all life on Earth has digested the legacy of information from its ancestral past to develop through time and reach its current state, was itself a gigantic cybernetic process. In other words, the processes of *thought* and *evolution* both follow the same rules. Because of this finding Bateson concluded that mind was *immanent* in nature. Bate-

son was not trying to prove the existence of the supernatural; rather, he wished merely to emphasize that this
"no-thing" we call information flows around in virtually all
biological processes in a strikingly similar fashion.

Bateson called this similarity "the pattern which connects," and in a private conversation a few years before his
death, he confessed that he believed the recognition and
study of this connecting pattern was the most important
development in Western thinking in the last 2,000 years.
Because of this he spent a good portion of his life trying to
teach his many students the importance of this pattern, and
he was always appalled when he saw others around him
teaching vast lists of facts by rote without teaching the
"glue" that holds such facts together. In *Mind and Nature* he
lamented, "Why do schools teach almost nothing of the
pattern which connects? Is it that teachers know that they
carry the kiss of death which will turn to tastelessness whatever they touch and therefore they are wisely unwilling to
touch or teach anything of real-life importance? Or is it that
they carry the kiss of death *because* they dare not teach anything of real-life importance?"[4]

Because it is the "no-thing" of information, or the pattern which connects, that seems to determine the most important aspects of a system, Bateson even suggested that
relationships, not objects, should be the basis of all definitions in science. He indicated that perhaps the right way to
begin to think about phenomena such as mind is not in
terms of the parts it is composed of, but more in terms of a
dance of interacting parts that is only secondarily pegged
down by the physical constraints of the system to which it
corresponds. This is, of course, the very idea about which
Searles expressed so much consternation.

Admittedly, it is a disturbing thing to think that parts are
less important to our understanding of things than something that is "no-thing." Be that as it may, it is not the only
disturbing implicaton of the functionalist approach. Once

one accepts this revelation and begins to reexamine the world with an eye trained to look for the pattern that connects, one quickly discovers that not only does the dance of the parts matter more in terms of definitions, but that the dance can also transcend its parts in terms of the effects it can have on the physical world.

## On Termite Nests and the Origin of Language

The classic example of the dance transcending its parts can be found in the lowly termite and the marvel of its nest. Dotting the bush country in Northern Australia are an endless array of huge stone monoliths, averaging a dozen feet square and only a few inches thick. The first thing noticeable about these tombstonelike mounds is that they all have a north-south orientation, which is why the insect responsible for their creation, the *Omitermes meridionalis*, is commonly known as the compass termite. The north-south orientation of these mounds is, of course, no accident. One of the requirements for the compass termite to live and perpetuate happily is that the temperature and humidity in its brooding chamber must be kept constant. Thus, in the early morning chill the most pressing need of the termite colony is to take in as much warmth as possible, and this is why the flat side of the mound faces the rising sun. At noon, when the sun shining down upon the outback is most intense, the most urgent requirement of the colony is to lose heat, and this is why only the knifelike edge of the monolith is exposed to the overhead sun.

This north-south orientation is not the only strategy the termite colony uses to control its temperature. The entire fortress is also honeycombed with thousands of ventilation shafts, and as the environmental conditions outside shift, thousands of termites scurry about, opening and closing valves as they control what is quite literally the air-conditioning system of their own version of a high-rise. In short, the architecture of this strange fortress is designed so that no matter how hotly the sun rains down or how vigorously the wind blows, the internal temperature and humidity of the mound remain the same.[5]

What is equally remarkable is that no single termite could ever accomplish such a miracle of engineering. A lone termite doesn't have an inkling how to go about altering the temperature of its environment. Even three or four termites gathered together are equally helpless. But keep adding termites one by one and sooner or later a sort of critical mass is reached, and as if the truth has suddenly dawned upon them, they gather into work crews and begin cementing grains of sand together with their saliva, building arches and connecting columns until the expertly designed fortress that will ultimately become their home grows like some strange flower around them.

Similarly, it has been discovered that even when the outside temperature is -28°F. and the humidity is 30 percent, the inside of a beehive remains warm, with 70° temperature and a humidity of 90 percent. The ability of a beehive to withstand high temperatures is equally impressive. In the 1950s, the German entomologist Martin Lindauer positioned a hive in full sunlight on a lava field near Salerno, Italy, where the air temperature was a staggering 158°F., and discovered that if the bees were allowed unlimited access to water, they could still keep the temperature in their brood chambers down to a hot but tolerable 95°F. by hanging the water in droplets and then fanning it with their wings throughout their hive.[6]

What is telling about this, what deserves to be contemplated for at least the length of an afternoon, is that the information contained in such an engineering marvel, the software, the dance of the parts, is quite beyond the capability of any solitary termite. Or as Harvard entomologist Edward O. Wilson puts it, "Animal aggregations alter their own physical environment to an extent disproportionately greater than the extent achieved by isolated individuals, and sometimes even in qualitatively novel ways."[7]

Such advanced pieces of software can be found in virtually all of the social insects. What is important to note about the software contained in the architecture and behavior of social insects such as termites and bees is that it originated with no single insect. There is no equivalent of an Imhotep or a Frank Lloyd Wright in the world of bees. In a very real sense, the software or marvelous information contained in such structures as the compass termite's fortress itself has grown and evolved in much the same way a living organism grows and evolves. And more than that, it has become more complex than any system any individual social insect could develop. The dance has transcended its parts.

The ability of this "no-thing" we call information to become organized in a way that transcends its parts is not limited to the insect world. Recently, linguist Derek Bickerton at the University of Hawaii has uncovered possible evidence of a similar piece of software evolving right in our own midst. The phenomena that Bickerton set out to study were so-called Creole languages, the mongrel ways of speaking that occasionally arise when one culture is forced to work together with great numbers of people speaking the language of an entirely different culture.

For example, when in 1875 the United States signed an exclusive trade agreement with the Hawaiian monarchy, the sugar industry in the islands began to boom, and workers poured in to man the sugar plantations. At first these workers, whose native tongues were Hawaiian, Korean, Japanese, and Spanish, spoke various "pidgeons"—makeshift and clumsy attempts at communication that employed the vocabulary of the English-speaking overseers mingled with whatever grammatical features were native to the tongue of the particular worker. As a consequence the various pidgeons comprised a sort of babel, with no grammatical features common to all of the workers.

However, Bickerton discovered that sometime between 1880 and 1910 the children of this first generation of adults suddenly began speaking an entirely new language, Hawaiian Creole, complete with its own syntactical sentence structure and grammatical rules. Although this new tongue borrowed words from all of the various languages represented in the workers, it was a brand-new language, incomprehensible to both the adults of the first generation and the English-speaking plantation owners.[8]

Bickerton's discovery does not end there. In studying the various other Creoles—more than a hundred are known— he has found that although the vocabularies vary, the syntactical sentence structure and grammatical rules present in Hawaiian Creole seem to be the same in all Creoles. Bickerton concludes that this similarity supports Noam Chomsky's theory that the ability to speak language is programmed into us.

Bickerton believes that the process that allowed Hawaiian Creole to blossom so quickly may be very similar to the process that enabled language to develop in the first place. In Bickerton's scenario, perhaps when our ancestors first came down from the trees and first began to wonder about things like the stars, what lies over the horizon, and death, something resembling Creole arose among them—or among their children. As succeeding generations of these novel-language–speaking hominids reproduced and spread, different environmental and cultural situations would have required different vocabularies, but Bickerton believes that the innate syntactical and grammatical substratum might have endured. He states, ''Biological language remained right where it was, while cultural language rode off in all directions."[9] Only in cases where a culture is uprooted, as with the Hawaiian sugar plantation workers, do these innate rules for ordering language come to the fore.

Given that it is doubtful any of the children of the Hawaiian plantation workers were aware of the grand linguistic design they were weaving around them, it seems that the dance has a certain life above and beyond its parts. Two intriguing questions arise from Bickerton's discovery. If, somewhere back in the mists of time, language itself arose as almost a self-evolving piece of software, as with termites, did it require a certain critical mass of children in order to spring into being? And perhaps more important, what other awesome pieces of software are this very moment dancing around us as we dodder on with our lives, completely unaware that we are its parts? At this point in time the first question must remain unanswered, although if Sheldrake's M-field hypothesis—and hence something resembling the hundredth monkey phenomenon—is proven correct, this may begin to provide us with a clue. As for the second question, in one way or another the rest of this book will be devoted to the tentative answer that various branches of science have posited.

Another implication that follows from the fact that the dance can often transcend its parts is that an examination of the parts alone may not immediately suggest the true complexity of the phenomenon embodied in the pattern that connects those parts. For example, in the case of Walter's robot tortoises, an examination of the few and relatively simple components comprising it—the photoelectric cell, motor, battery, and electrical contact—does not immediately suggest to us that, when put together, this simple conglomeration can display such complex and seemingly ineffable qualities as moodiness and impatience.

Our inability to recognize the disproportionate state of affairs that can often exist between the dance and its parts has long been a hindrance to our understanding of many biological phenomena, especially when it comes to assessing decision making and/or intelligent capabilities of organisms other than ourselves. For example, the lowly crayfish has but 90,000 neurons—a seemingly scant number compared to the 10 billion or so we humans possess. Because of this, for many years scientists believed that the crayfish's limited neural circuitry meant that its decision-making capability would be correspondingly limited. It was thought that the crayfish's neural capacity certainly wasn't complex enough to allow it to do two things at once; if it was performing one activity, that activity would cease when another was stimulated. However, in 1984 UCLA researchers Kirstie Bellman and Franklin Krasne learned that the crayfish can quite easily do two seemingly incompatible things at once, such as feeding and escaping from a net. Krasne concluded, "They take a larger domain of things into account, which we hadn't thought possible before."[10]

Such disparity between the dance and its parts becomes even more striking in organisms with even simpler neural systems. I have in my home a saltwater aquarium in which I keep, among other things, a number of sea anemones, those eerie flowerlike animals related to jellyfish, which biologists know as *coelenterates*. Sea anemones have no brains, nor even a ganglionic or concentrated mass of nerve cells that might function as a central control. In addition to the anemone's meager neural equipment, biologists have found that each of its chrysanthemumlike tentacles possesses its own separate memory.

For instance, when a small piece of filter paper is soaked in beef broth, any given tentacle will accept it readily, placing it in the anemone's mouth until all of the beef broth is removed, and then the anemone will spit the paper back out again. However, if a tentacle is given a plain piece of filter paper, the first time such an offering is made the tentacle will accept the paper and go through the same procedure. But once it discovers that there is nothing in the paper, the particular tentacle in question will not accept an "empty" piece of filter paper again. This learned ability to discriminate between pieces of paper, however, is possessed only by the tentacle that has actually gone through the process. The anemone's other tentacles must learn the skill for themselves, and even then, it seems, each tentacle's memory only retains the information for about fifteen minutes before it "forgets" and must go through the entire learning procedure once again.[11]

This suggests that the anemone is a victim of the simplicity of its parts, and this is no doubt correct to a certain extent, but it is quickly tempered by some of the anemone's other abilities. I also have in my tank a rather large anemone about nine inches across known as a carpet anemone, and if I drop it a small piece of cooked fish and one side of the anemone fails to snatch it up properly with its hundreds of small waving tentacles, the other side of the anemone quickly curls up to the rescue. Somehow the so-called mindless anemone, without brain or even a ganglionic concentration of nerves, manages to coordinate all of its parts. Arguably, all of the carpet anemone's many hundreds of tentacles with their equally numerous and separate memories have no more "idea" that they are part of a coordinated activity than do the children of the sugar plantation workers who came up with Hawaiian Creole. But that doesn't seem to matter to the level of the anemone at which its activity becomes coordinated. It's dancing its own particular dance.

For all of its apparent anatomical handicaps, the anemone at least possesses neurons. However, if we arrange all animal life on Earth in a hierarchy according to the complexity of their nervous systems (and let it be said right here that arranging things into hierarchies and then trying to draw meaningful conclusions from those hierarchies is, at best, risky business), the anemone is generally recognized as the last animal on the scale to possess a true nervous system. As we continue on down this so-called ladder of life, none of the organisms we encounter even possess neurons. But that does not stop the dance.

Many single-celled animals such as protozoa have well-coordinated cilia, or hairlike filaments, that enable them to move quite gracefully through the water. My favorite among these is a little creature known as *Mixotricha paradoxa* (see Figure 13). Biologists describe *Mixotricha paradoxa* as possessing an "extreme smoothness" of movement, and what makes this particular dance of parts all the more remarkable is that not only is *Mixotricha paradoxa* without a nervous system to coordinate its slow ballet, but if one looks closely at its perfectly coordinated cilia, one finds that they are not true appendages but are themselves separate organisms, rod-like bacteria that have attached themselves to the protozoan and provide it with mobility in exchange for the benefit of being part of a microbial cartel. Biologists call such a working relationship between dissimilar organisms who have massed together for the greater good of all *symbiosis*. What makes *Mixotricha paradoxa* such a splendid little object lesson on life is that it is itself part of a larger symbiotic relationship, for *Mixotricha paradoxa* is found only in the gut of a particular kind of termite. In exchange for its warm home, the *Mixotricha paradoxa* provides the termite with a much needed service, since it is only the protozoan, and not the termite, that is able to digest and convert wood into a usable food source.[12]

Despite their total lack of a nervous system, protozoa are also able to both learn and remember. In a test similar to the beef broth experiment with the anemone, researchers have found that when a protozoan known as the slipper animalcule is offered an indigestible granule of carbon, it will accept it only once, and if it encounters such a granule again it will ignore it. Intriguingly, it has been found that the slipper animalcule's memory, like the anemone's, lasts only about fifteen minutes.[13]

Down still further the dance continues, and even bacte-

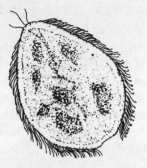

FIGURE 13    *The* Mixotricha paradoxa. *Each of the cilia or hairlike organs on its side is a separate organism.*

ria, it seems, are able to process information in ways that belie the orthodox belief that they are simple organisms. For example, the intestinal bacterium *E. coli* is able to process information about twenty different chemical substances in its environment at the same time, and not only does it swim in the direction where it senses more nutrient, but it swims in the direction where the amount of nutrient is increasing at the fastest rate. And if this is not enough, as it does this it reevaluates the complex chemical makeup of its environment every four seconds. The incredible information-processing abilities of the *E. coli* has even inspired F. Eugene Yates, director of UCLA's Crump Institute for Medical Engineering, to suggest that living bacteria may someday be incorporated into digital computers—as he puts it, "marrying the best features of biology and electronics."[14]

The information-processing abilities of microorganisms becomes most striking, however, when they come together to take part in a larger dance. The classic example of this involves an amoebalike creature known as *Dictyostelium*, or slime mold. When environmental conditions are favorable, the *Dictyostelium* spends its life as an individual, foraging happily for bacteria in the leaf mulch of hardwood forests. The *Dictyostelium* is a solitary sort, in competition with the others of its kind, whom it will occasionally even eat. In this state the individual *Dictyostelium* reproduces every few hours by simple cell division. Sometimes, however, perhaps when food becomes scarce, the *Dictyostelium* will stop and begin to send out a chemical signal. Soon other *Dictyostelia* heed its call and converge on the original sender, all the while sending out their own chemical beacons, until tens of thousands gather en masse.

When about 100,000 have gathered, the *Dictyostelia* cling to one another and begin to move about as if they were now a single organism, a tiny slug about one twenty-fifth of an inch long. The slug wriggles up through the leaf mulch until it reaches the sunlight, and then the many thousands of *Dictyostelia* comprising the new organism undergo an even more radical change. Some of them grow into a stalk that reaches up into the air, while others at the top of the stalk turn themselves into spores (see Figure 14). At the top of the stalk the spores wait until the wind carries them off to better hunting grounds, where they once again become individual *Dictyostelia* wandering through the leaf mulch by themselves.[15]

As we have seen, the complex information embodied in the architecture of a termite mound reveals quite clearly that the dance can transcend its parts. The fact that it takes a certain critical mass of termites to cause such a complex piece of software to pop into being has caused some researchers to suggest that perhaps the termite colony itself should be thought of as a single organism. In the case of *Dictyostelium* the question of what comprises an individual organism becomes even more puzzling.

*Dictyostelium* is not the only creature that possesses such a dubious nature. For example, *Labyrinthula* is a tiny marine organism that is quite happy to spend its life as a single-celled creature. It is also just as happy to band together occasionally with others of its kind and becoming a larger creature and move through tubelike structures in the larger

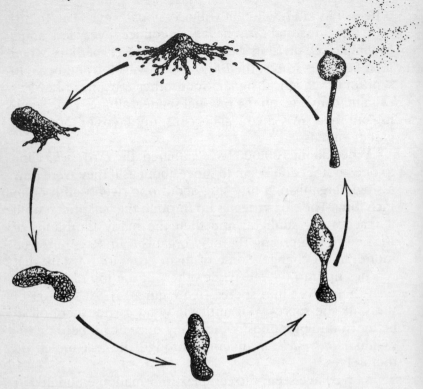

FIGURE 14   *The slime mold. Nature's perfect example of the dance transcending its parts.*

and now free-swimming collective, almost like corpuscles through a circulatory system.[16] And if this ambiguity between what is an individual and what is a collective seems somewhat far removed from life at our own human level of existence, recently it has been suggested that slime molds are not the only things that microorganisms can mass together to create.

## THE HUMAN BRAIN AS A SYMBIOTIC COLONY OF BACTERIA

Boston University microbiologist Lynn Margulis has long held that symbiosis has played a major role in biological evolution, and this belief has led her to advance a number of remarkable theories. For example, in each of the cells in our body are little subunits known as *mitochondria,* which are responsible for the cell's ability to metabolize fat. Mitochondria also possess their own DNA, which is quite unlike the DNA found in the rest of the cell. For years this fact remained a mystery, but in the early 1970s Margulis proposed an explanation. She believes that at some point in evolution mitochondria were free-swimming bacteria that danced their way into our ancient one-celled ancestors, and points out that symbiotic relationships of bacteria living in one-celled host organisms can still be found in nature today.[17]

Although Margulis' theories were at first greeted with skepticism, in recent years they have gained wider acceptance. In particular, her notion that mitochondria started as free-swimming bacteria recently received a boost when it was discovered that not only is their DNA different from that in the rest of the cell, but it isn't even written in the same genetic code.[18]

Mitochondria are not the only components of our bodies that Margulis believes are of symbiotic origin. She believes that the hairlike tail that allows human sperm to move also began, at some point in evolution, just as the cilia in *Mixotricha paradoxa,* as a free-swimming bacterium known as a *spirochete.* In her 1981 book *Symbiosis and Cell Evolution* Margulis points out that such symbiotic relationships are still occurring between spirochetes and some microorganisms. As further evidence, she also points out that some spirochetes are built out of a specific protein structure known as a microtubule, and that the same distinctive microtubular structure is found in many places throughout the biological world—in the cell whips that allow our chromosomes to move around during cell division, in the cilia lining our lungs, in the receptor cells that allow us to taste, smell, maintain our balance, and even in the light-sensitive rod cells in the retinas in our eyes.[19]

Margulis' most astounding assertion, however, is that even our brains are the result of an ancient microbial dance of parts, perhaps not too terribly dissimilar from the dance that allows the *Dictyostelia* to come together to form a larger organism.[20] She bases this belief on the fact that our nervous systems, our axons and dendrites, are composed of the same distinctive microtubular structure as the corkscrew tails of some of the earth's most ancient bacterial forms.[21] In short, she has offered evidence that the biological component of our minds is itself perhaps the crowning phase of bacterial evolution.

Thus, in a way we have come full circle. Not only are we humans part of a larger dance, but human evolution may be the result of a dance. The fact that we carry within our bodies certain structures that seem more related to primitive free-swimming bacteria than to complex human form gives new meaning to the discovery that the salinity of human blood is very close to the salinity of the ocean. It is said that life began in the ocean, and in a certain sense it seems that we still carry the ancient seas around within us. Or as Margulis puts it, "Basically, we're made of bacteria and we are containers for bacteria."[22]

Margulis' symbiotic theory of the origin of life once again raises the question of precisely what it means to be a sentient individual. If each of us is the end result of a symbiotic colony of bacteria, when we speak of ourselves should we say "I" or should we say "we"? In tackling this question one is once again reminded of Bohm's assertion that many of the terms we use to describe the world are merely semantic conventions that we "abstract" out of the seamless web of nature, and reality is an unbroken whole in which phenomena such as individual organisms are no more separate from that whole than individual subatomic particles.

In this sense, the question What is an individual organism? is similar to Bohm's wondering if an oxygen molecule inside a cell should be considered alive but ceases to be alive once it has passed through the cell wall and out into the air. In other words, the question of what differentiates one individual organism from the next is similar to the question of what it is that differentiates living matter from nonliving matter. It is, in short, a question of boundaries. Throughout his life Gregory Bateson believed that the boundary between living and nonliving things was distinct. Some scientists, however, are moving away from this point of view. And as we will see, the definition of life that scientists are arriving at—like the functionalist's definition of mind—once again has less to do with the substance of a living thing's parts, and more to do with the "no-thing" of the dance.

## WHAT IS LIFE?

To a nonscientist, the difference between living and nonliving things seems obvious. Human beings and lilac bushes are alive and rocks and pieces of glass are not. However, in spite of the fact that it seems easy to recognize the fundamental differences between a blue whale and a blob of mercury, biologists have found that it is not so easy to formulate a precise definition of life.

The dictionary defines life as those things which have the ability to function, grow, and reproduce, and yet crystals also exhibit all of these traits. Are crystals alive? More accurate definitions include references to other usual traits of living organisms, such as movement, responsiveness, and exchange of gases and nutrients with the environment. But even if these are taken into account, problems still arise. For example, Oriental lotus seeds carbon-dated as 2,000 years old have been successfully germinated and grown. And yet during their 2,000-year-old slumber they exhibit none of these characteristics. Similarly, through a process known as cryptobiosis some animals are able to survive almost total dehydration. One such creature is a small water animal known as a rotifer. A colony of rotifers can be completely dried out and kept in a state of suspended animation for years. But as soon as water is added to them they come back to life. One story has it that a dry chunk of moss, which had spent 120 years in a museum, still yielded living rotifers when rewetted.[23] Again, are rotifers alive when they are in their dehydrated state? And if phenomena such as cryptobiosis can occur in the universe, what sort of definition might we arrive at that would enable us to recognize even more unusual forms of life in the universe?

To remedy the problems that arise when one tries to formulate a precise definition of life, Columbia University physicist Gerald Feinberg and New York University biochemist Robert Shapiro recently banded together to tackle the matter. In their 1980 book *Life Beyond Earth* they offer a possible solution, stating that because all life on Earth is so complexly interlocked, little distinction can be made between life and nonlife and that the best definition of life is the entire Earth itself, what they call the "biosphere."

This idea in itself is not new. Lynn Margulis and British chemist James Lovelock have also proposed that Earth itself functions as if it were a gigantic living organism, in their "Gaia hypothesis"—named after Gaia, the Greek goddess of Earth. As evidence, they cite the fact that, like the various types of cybernetic systems studied by Bateson, Earth self-regulates itself. For instance, during the past four billion years, the Sun's energy output has increased significantly, and yet temperatures in Earth's lower atmosphere, like the temperature in a beehive, have not risen correspondingly. Similarly, the oxygen content of Earth's atmosphere has re-

mained remarkably stable. Why? Margulis and Lovelock believe that all life on Earth works together to regulate and
maintain its relatively stable environment.[24] In other words,
climate, the chemical makeup of the atmosphere, and many
of the other elements that make Earth so hospitable to life
as we know it are all the products of a dance of many parts.

The second important distinction that Feinberg and Shapiro make between life and nonlife is even more startling.
Given that the same general kinds of chemical and physical
processes take place in both living and nonliving things,
they conclude that the best definition of life should be based
not on a study of what parts comprise an organism (that is,
nucleic acids and proteins), but on the amount of order
present in the arrangement of those parts (defining order as
a measure of how likely any given arrangement of parts is
to have occurred by chance.)[25] What is interesting is that for
some time now science has known that order is just another
way of referring to how much information is encoded in a
system. In other words, in Feinberg and Shapiro's view,
what we define as alive, like the functionalist's definition of
consciousness, should not be based on the measurement of
a substance or an energy (say, any proposed "life force")
but on a measure of pure information.

Feinberg and Shapiro point out that taken to its logical
conclusion, such a definition forces one to consider the possibility of life on other planets based on ammonia, petro-
leum, and even liquid helium. They consider the possibility
of living balloons, airborne organisms filled with hydrogen,
floating in the upper atmosphere of Jupiter and microorganisms composed of polymer on Mars. If the quintessence
of life is order or pure information they point out that there
may be no corner of the cosmos that does not possess some
form of life. Living organisms composed entirely of radiant
energy may inhabit the depths of interstellar clouds, and
plasma life, organized patterns of magnetic force, may bask
in the upper surfaces of stars.[26]

However, above and beyond the mind-boggling aspects of such speculations, the most profound assertion made by Feinberg and Shapiro is not in the specifics of life forms they ponder, but their conclusion that the most intrinsic difference between a cocker spaniel and a lump of coal is not something as tangible and readily defined as a DNA molecule or a type of amino acid. It is something that is "nothing," that mysterious nonentity we call information.

Surely some monumental synthesis is at hand, with many thinkers from many different directions asserting the primacy of information over matter and energy. I believe that such a synthesis is slowly taking place in the world of science, and that the resulting increase this synthesis will provide in our understanding of the way that information functions in the warp and weft of the universe may even show us the way to ultimately penetrate the worlds that lie beyond the quantum.

Time and again throughout this chapter we have seen that one of the most important elements of the dance is its ability to self-organize. For example, it seems difficult to fathom that any lone *Dictyostelium* formulated the means to direct 100,000 of its kind to form a collective that functions as a single organism. It is similarly unlikely that any single culturally uprooted child creates a Creole tongue; that any single termite designs a nest; that any given tentacle on an anemone knows how to coordinate the movement of the whole; that any individual organism on Earth can regulate and maintain the climate and atmosphere of the entire planet; or that any solitary bacterium decided to come together with billions of its kind to form a human brain.

The dance has a life of its own, and even more importantly, in living that life it displays a most extraordinary talent—the ability to curl in upon itself, to not only maintain its own existence, but to increase and grow in complexity, becoming ever more intricate, diverse, and packed with more of its own essence, more information.

For a good portion of the history of science this ability of the dance to self-organize has largely been ignored. However, in the past decade there has been a growing flurry of interest in self-organizing phenomena, and significant headway has been made in unraveling the mysterious laws that seem to govern such self-organization. One researcher responsible for a good deal of this sudden interest is the Nobel Prize–winning chemist Ilya Prigogine.

## THE SELF-ORGANIZING UNIVERSE

One reason science has neglected the phenomenon of self-organization for so long is because of its reverence for one of its most dearly embraced rules, a formidable dictum known as the second law of thermodynamics. In its simplest terms, this law states that, over time, closed systems tend toward greater states of disorder—a drop of ink in a beaker of water becomes more dispersed; rooms tend to become messier, not cleaner; and mountains are steadily worn down by the wind and pulverized into sand.

The first formulation of the second law of thermodynamics was made by the French physicist Sadi Carnot in 1824. Carnot based his conclusion that systems tend toward greater states of disorder on his observations of a heat engine. Given that the engine—and machines in general—tend ultimately toward breakdown, and given that the Industrial Revolution was in full swing and the universe at large as well as most of the phenomena in it were viewed as little more than machines, Carnot—and the generations of scientists who followed him and who honed and added to his original observation—concluded that the second law of thermodynamics must apply to the rest of the universe as well.

There is, of course, one glaring problem. Nonmechanical living organisms do not conform so neatly to Carnot's law. If we examine the fossil record and trace life back to its microbial beginnings on Earth, we find that organizations of cells, far from drifting apart and becoming more dispersed, came together in increasingly more intricate designs. The origin of the DNA molecule itself, with all its staggering complexities, posed the most striking problem to the sanctity of the second law of thermodynamics. The scientific establishment reacted by stating that biological life on Earth was an aberration, a temporary backwater that will ultimately be destroyed as the river of time carries the rest of the universe ever onward in its inexorable march toward disorder.

It wasn't until 1945, when the Austrian physicist Erwin Schrödinger published a series of papers under the title "What is Life?" that researchers began to feel even vaguely comfortable about wondering if there could be some further reconciliation between the second law of thermodynamics and the apparent biological drive toward complexity. One such researcher was Ilya Prigogine. Prigogine became convinced that if life really arises out of a primordial soup, there had to be more to understanding how it succeeded in going against the second law of thermodynamics than just labeling such a feat a temporary aberration.

Because Prigogine's idea went against the accepted wisdom, many of his colleagues tried to dissuade him, suggesting that he confine his studies to how disorder, not order, wins out in the universe.[27] In spite of this, Prigogine remained convinced that there were undiscovered laws to describe how life arose out of chaos. One of the first encouraging signs that he might be correct came when he encountered a phenomenon known as the Benard Instability. The Benard Instability occurs when a liquid is heated from below. It has been found that as the temperature in such a heated liquid rises, at a certain point molecules in the liquid suddenly "self-organize," arranging themselves into hexagonal cells that structurally resemble the panes in a miniature stained-glass window. The Benard Instability intrigued Prigogine because the way that currents of heated liquid pass around and through such cells was not dissimilar to processes occurring in living cells. Prigogine concluded that if such a dramatic example of self-organization was possible in fluid dynamics, it should also be possible in chemistry and biology.[28]

For years Prigogine worked on a mathematical understanding that might explain such spontaneous self-organization in processes other than heated liquids, but it wasn't until the late sixties that a Russian biophysicist named Anatoli Zhabotinsky discovered a chemical reaction that precisely fulfilled the predictions made by Prigogine's equations. What Zhabotinsky discovered was that when certain chemical substances were mixed together in a liquid state, instead of becoming murky and dispersed they oscillated back and forth with clocklike precision between two different and distinct states. This effect, called the Zhabotinsky Reaction, becomes most distinct when an indicator dye is added to the mixture, since a container of such liquid will turn red and then blue and then red again, and so on.[29] At last, Prigogine had an example of what he meant by a more ordered state arising out of apparent disorder.

No longer confined to vague generalizations about the possibility of self-organizing systems, Prigogine was able to refine his equations even further and offer a totally new understanding of thermodynamic processes. Given that most systems we know of are *open* and are constantly exchanging energy or matter and, perhaps most importantly, exchanging *information* with their environment, Prigogine observed that all such systems should be viewed as fluctuating. At times such fluctuations may become so powerful that a preexisting level of organization in a system cannot withstand the fluctuation. Prigogine called this moment of crisis for a system a "bifurcation point" and believed that when such a point is reached, a system has two options. Either it will be destroyed by the fluctuation and disintegrate into chaos, or it will suddenly leap to an entirely new level of organization, a new internal order that Prigogine called a "dissipative structure" (because it is the role of this new level of organization to "dissipate" the influx of energy, matter, and/or information responsible for the disabling fluctuation). It was for his theory of such dissipative structures that Prigogine won the 1977 Nobel Prize.[30]

Inherent in Prigogine's view are several startling implications. The first is Prigogine's belief that self-organizing chemical processes such as the Zhabotinsky Reaction are midway between life and nonlife. Moreover, far from being aberrations, Prigogine believed that such self-organizing systems may be the norm in the universe, and closed systems such as those described by the second law of thermodynamics may well be the aberrant phenomenon. Last, and perhaps most remarkable of all, is Prigogine's conclusion that disorder is not an ultimate fate from which nothing can escape, but is actually the progenitor of order. In this sense, Prigogine set the second law of thermodynamics on its ear and completely reversed one of the most long-held assumptions of classical physics.[31]

In short, in self-organizing phenomena such as the Zhabotinsky Reaction we have evidence of an entirely new property of matter. Not only can people and protozoa join hands to take part in the dance, but molecules can also. As Prigogine stated, "The amazing thing is that each molecule knows in some way what the other molecules will do at the same time, over relatively macroscopic distances. These experiments provide examples of the ways in which molecules communicate. . . . That is a property everybody always accepted in living systems, but in nonliving systems it was quite unexpected."[32]

In his 1984 book *Order Out of Chaos*, coauthored with the chemist Isabelle Stengers, Prigogine offers what he feels is the inescapable conclusion. Biological life, instead of being a pocket of strangeness gazing out at a cold and sterile universe, is embedded in a living universe. In other words, we are no different in kind from the sand beneath our feet and the clouds over our heads. We are cut from the same cloth, and everywhere, in every corner of its fabric, the cloth is involved in the dance. As Prigogine states, "This is the heart of the message . . . in my book. Matter is not inert. It is alive and active."[33]

Prigogine's work has had a galvanizing effect on scientific thinking and is in part responsible for a recent flurry of interest in the study of disorder and chaos in general. Researchers in branches of science from meteorology to mathematics are discovering still further examples of self-organizing phenomena, and many scientists believe that unraveling the hidden rules and patterns that still lurk in the once unassailable mists of chaos may emerge as the next big revolution in physics.

Suffice it to say there are many examples of self-organizing phenomena in the world we perceive around us, and no doubt many more waiting to be both discovered and deciphered. For example, on a desolate part of Spitzbergen, an island north of Norway, it has been known for years that the stones on the beach arrange themselves in a remarkable honeycomblike network. The circles in the network range in size from a few feet, where they are surrounded by pebbles, to several yards in diameter, where boulders sometimes mark their borders. The notion that pranksters might be responsible for moving the rocks has been eliminated, and scientists do not yet know the natural forces responsible for this disarming pattern, but it is known that whatever they are, they occur rather rapidly, for scientists disrupting the pattern one year have returned the following spring to find the rocks replaced neatly in the borders.[34]

Similarly, there is a growing consensus among cosmologists that galaxies themselves also link together into a subtle network of filaments and voids that gravitational forces alone do not seem capable of explaining.[35] As we have seen, recent definitions of life such as that offered by Feinberg and

Shapiro already suggest that living and nonliving things belong on a continuum in which the only real difference is a measure of information or order. It may be that as our understanding of living processes becomes more sophisticated we will come to recognize that the patterned stones of Spitzbergen Island and the filamentary structure of the universe at large are also inherently biological. As with so many of the dichotomies in our lives—the distinction between good and evil, the strict division between male and female cultural roles—perhaps a clear dividing line between living and nonliving things does not strictly exist. Instead of an either/or way of looking at things, perhaps we should recognize that the quality of being alive is a matter of degree or approach. Perhaps the stone circles of Spitzbergen Island are simply a different form of life than we are.

All this said, I am now ready to advance my boldest heresy. I believe that the poltergeist that manifested itself in my youth was also such a piece of software, a self-organized dance of interacting parts. Perhaps those parts were the neurons in my own brain. Perhaps they also included the neurons in the brains of one or more individuals around me. Or perhaps the parts involved a collection of things of which I am not even aware.

Whatever the case, I do not believe the poltergeist possessed any more substance or energy as we know them than either consciousness or life. I believe that, like the architecture of a termite mound, the pattern behind the creation of Hawaiian Creole, and the design inherent in the collectivity of *Dictyostelia*, for the moment the poltergeist must be spoken of as existing only in the realm of pure information. I believe this not only because sincere parapsychological effort has failed to uncover any evidence of material or energetic processes at work in its manifestations, but more because, like the dart of the honeybee as it constructs its hive and the perfectly coordinated undulations of the *Mixo-*

*tricha paradoxa's* cilia, it too unerringly possesses the hall-marks of the dance.

If I am right in my surmise, just as we may create a termite mound by putting together a critical mass of termites or create a Creole language by transplanting a group of children in a culture whose tongue they do not speak, given the proper assemblage of parts it should also be possible to create a poltergeist. Surprisingly, about a decade ago this was done by a Canadian psychical research group headed by parapsychologist A. R. G. Owen.

## CONJURING UP PHILIP

A. R. G. Owen first became interested in poltergeist phenomena when he was asked to write a review of the available literature on the subject. In the course of this endeavor he became personally involved in the study of a poltergeist haunting, centering around a young Scottish girl named Virginia Campbell. He became so convinced of the validity of the paranormal nature of the phenomenon that he ended up writing what has come to be one of the recognized classics on poltergeist hauntings, a 1964 work entitled *Can We Explain the Poltergeist?* In the fall of 1972, eight of Owen's friends, including his wife Iris, decided to attempt to "create" their own ghost.

To make sure that they weren't conjuring up an actual spirit, they carefully designed their ghost by sitting around in a circle and creating details of their own ghost, person by person, until they had collectively come up with a purely fictional character. One person decided that the ghost would be male and his name would be Philip; the next person decided that Philip would be an aristocratic Englishman living in the seventeenth century during the time of Oliver Cromwell; the next person decided that he was married to a cold and uncaring wife named Dorothea; and so forth, until they not only had created every detail of Philip's physical appearance but also his likes and dislikes, the sort of food he ate, and even the details of his extramarital affair with a raven-haired Gypsy girl named Margo. As a further precautionary measure, the group also incorporated into Philip's story certain historical details that were totally fictional and contrary to actual historical events.

All this done, the group then arranged to meet once a week and hold séances in order to "contact" their totally manufactured ghost. The group met for a year, sitting around a table with their hands flat on its surface, with absolutely no results. In their 1976 book on the experience, *Conjuring Up Philip*, Iris Owen and Margaret Sparrow wrote that the group became so discouraged that they were almost ready to quit.

It was then that Iris Owen came across an article by C. Brookes-Smith, D. W. Hunt, and K. J. Batcheldor in the *Journal of the Society for Physical Research* describing a similar series of experiments that Batcheldor and his associates had undertaken in England. In their own work, Batcheldor's group had hoped mainly to produce specific physical phenomena such as table rapping, and to this end had also met for regular séances. However, instead of assuming an air of solemnity at their séances, Batcheldor's group had adopted a different method. Batcheldor and his associates discovered that during Victorian times the séance circles that reported the most unusual results were not lugubrious and candlelit ceremonies, but gay and festive social events in which the participants sat around talking, telling jokes, and generally enjoying themselves as if they were expecting nothing to happen. Batcheldor and his group reported that they began to obtain unusual results only when they too adopted a similar air of conviviality.

Encouraged, the Owen group no longer sat around their table in silent meditation, but began joking and laughing and even singing songs, and a few sessions into this new method, to their amazement, "Philip" suddenly started to communicate with them by causing loud raps to emanate from the table's surface. They quickly established a code of one rap for yes and two for no, and in no time, to their continued astonishment, were carrying on regular conversations with their tailor-made ghost.

True to character, Philip answered questions in a manner quite consistent with the story they had created for him. For example, as the group had decided that Philip's wife Dorothea was a less than pleasant person, so Philip readily agreed, even making scratching sounds instead of raps whenever Dorothea's name was mentioned. Philip also incorporated all of the historical inaccuracies in his fictional biography into his answers.

However, like any proper dance, Philip also transcended his parts, adding twists and turns to his story that his creators had not anticipated. For example, when on one occasion he was asked about his Gypsy mistress, Margo, Philip asserted that, contrary to what the group had thought, he had never really loved her. Philip also elaborated greatly on his life's story, informing the group that his parents had died of smallpox. He talked about his fondness for hunting and revealed that he kept peregrines, shot deer with a musket, and preferred human beaters to dogs when hunting game birds. He also described in detail his work as a spy on behalf of Charles I in fighting against Cromwell's armies.

Philip also displayed a distinct personality. Like Walter's robot tortoises, he was moody. He developed affinities with certain members of the group and would respond to their questions more readily than to those of others. He enjoyed jokes and would cause the table to rattle vigorously when he was amused. He liked some songs—"Rock-a-Bye Baby" was one of his favorites—and would get angry if the group tried to sing certain others. He was impatient and childlike and disliked being ignored. If the group became distracted in conversation and neglected him for too long, he started to rap repeatedly until he once again gained their attention. However, he did not like being grilled too continuously, and most of all he did not like to be threatened. Once, when Philip was being uncooperative and one of the members of the group warned him that they could send him away and replace him with somebody else, Philip got angry and vanished, and it took several hours of coaxing to get him to return.

What is intriguing is that so much of the Philip phenomenon is noticeably similar to my own experiences with the poltergeist. For example, like the poltergeist, Philip was mischievous and childlike, and like the poltergeist, he communicated primarily through disembodied raps and sometimes scratching sounds (another often reported occurrence in the literature on poltergeist hauntings*). In the case of my own poltergeist, the raps usually came from the ceiling, walls, or windows. In the Philip experiment, the raps first emanated from the table, but they subsequently emanated from the walls as well. In this regard, it is interesting to note that the Owen group often recorded their sessions and had Philip's raps analyzed by an acoustic engineer named Alan Gauld. Gauld discovered that not only did the rise and fall of the volume of the sound in Philip's raps "differ noticeably from that in ordinary percussion raps," but in spite of their loudness were also incredibly short in duration, lasting only 0.16 second, or about a third as long as the sounds humans are able to make when they rap the table with their knuckles or feet.[36]

* The Owen group describes Philip's scratching as sounding like fingernails drawing across the underside of the table, and my own poltergeist also occasionally employed this method of communication. For example, once when I was in college and had my own apartment, a visiting and skeptical friend challenged the poltergeist to do something, whereupon it sounded as if someone placed their nails on one end of the living room ceiling and slowly drew them across the entire length of the ceiling—about sixteen feet—as my friend gazed upward in disbelief, his doubt evaporating.

Philip's mischievous nature and his rappings were not the only paranormal behavior he exhibited. As the sessions continued, Philip became stronger and actually started moving the table around the room, causing it to dance on one leg and even move up the walls. During this time the members of the group kept their hands flat against the tabletop, but Philip demonstrated that he was also capable of moving things when no one was touching them. Glasses of lemonade and ashtrays inadvertently left on the table would suddenly tip over or slide off, but small gifts offered to Philip would remain mysteriously in place, even when Philip tipped the table at precarious angles. One member of the group even reported that after one session he returned home to find his own tables and chairs moved about.

Perhaps the most astounding aspect of Philip was that he allowed his activities to be filmed. Having caught wind of the strange goings-on in the Owens household, the Canadian Broadcasting Corporation paid the group a visit in November of 1973, and there, with sound and camera crew milling about and blazing arc lights and videotape going, Philip not only continued his rapping undaunted but actually seemed to show off a bit, dancing the table merrily around the room.

In the time since, Philip has been the subject of several Canadian documentaries and has also performed for live studio audiences for Canadian television. On one of these occasions, Philip—who usually manifested himself at the table around which the group was sitting—actually seemed miffed that he had not been placed on the platform where most of the other of the show's guests were located. Owen and Sparrow wrote in their book:

It was soon obvious that Philip felt that his place was up on the platform with the moderator and the panelists. The table tried every way to get on to that platform—there were three overhanging steps up to the platform. It took quite a while, and a fair

amount of maneuvering before it managed it. The whole procedure was hilarious, and the camera crews succeeded in filming the
entire proceeding. Philip had to indulge in some quite complicated
positionings with the legs of the table in order to climb onto the
platform. Once there, it made straight for the moderator, who was
asked by one of the group to say hello to Philip. He looked somewhat doubtful, but did as requested, placed his hand on the table,
and said, "Hello, Philip." He was obviously surprised, as were the
television crew and audience, when a very loud rap came in reply
right underneath his hand. He continued to ask questions and to
receive raps in reply. These were all recorded and filmed. The
program was televised over the Toronto City TV system and was
broadcast in Toronto, on the program "World of the Unexplained."[37]

It is important to mention that in spite of his seemingly individual personality, Philip's existence ultimately appeared to be dependent on the minds of the individuals
present at any given session. For example, if Philip was
asked a historical question to which no member of the group
knew the answer—or for which the group had not collectively formulated an incorrect answer—he was also unable
to provide an answer to the question. Similarly, his tastes in
jokes and songs changed slightly when the composition of
the group changed. And if several of the attending members
of the group happened to be recovering from an illness,
Philip's raps were also correspondingly feeble. Why Philip
was unable to answer some questions but occasionally gave
original answers to others remains a mystery. However, one
possible answer is that since Philip was always, at least in
part, an amalgam of the group's collective opinions, it may
be that on an unconscious level the group *had* unwittingly
formed a consensus response to those questions to which
Philip gave seemingly original answers.

Whatever the case, the fact that Philip was able to answer questions in a coherent fashion at all is remarkable. It
is also perhaps a process that has been used before in certain

cultures. For example, in Tanzania the Safwa people have long employed a ritual similar to the way the Toronto group conjured up Philip, to cause a chair to stand still or shake in response to questions put to it by the sitter. Just as F. Eugene Yates has suggested the building of computers with living bacteria as parts, perhaps someday we will build computers sensitive to quantum events easily controlled by psychokinesis and imbue them with the breath of life by instilling poltergeists such as Philip into their circuitry.

In any case, Philip seems to me markedly similar to symbiotic collectives such as those found in the marine microorganism *Labyrinthula*—something more than its assembled parts, but something equally dependent on those parts for its existence. And like the other dances we have examined in this chapter, those traits that make Philip more than just the sum of his parts—his distinct personality, moods, and unpredictable nature—organized themselves at some level and in some way of which his parts were not immediately cognizant. One of the implications of Philip's ability to self-organize out of a collective of human consciousnesses is that perhaps the border that divides one consciousness from the next is not so terribly absolute, but is more like the border that defines one globule of mercury from the next. Just as a group of mercury globules can come together and meld to form a larger globule, perhaps the consciousnesses that brought Philip into existence took part in a similar melding. The process also seems to work in reverse. For example, just as a group of cells in a developing embryo can self-organize and develop into identical twins when divided, it seems that certain fluctuations in an individual's personality, such as extreme trauma in childhood, can cause a bifurcation point to be reached and this personality can divide and self-organize into a group of intact personalities to create the phenomenon we know of as multiple personality.

Biologist Lewis Thomas has said that the self is a complex dialogue among internal voices. I agree with him, and

I would like to add that to a certain extent our mental experience suggests that even these voices self-organize into subordinate wholes not unlike the separate organisms that come together to form a symbiotic protozoan. Who can deny that a bad habit, once it is fully established, is not as willful and quasi-independent as Philip seems to be? Or that an addiction or a worry does not take on a life of its own? Or that even a talent possesses a seeming desire to assert itself, to be nourished and further developed? Just as Philip disliked being ignored for too long, these voices squabble with each other and vie for the focus of our attention and, indeed, much of the current stage of human development seems devoted to learning how to manage this both terrible and glorious chatter.

Bateson believed that there must be an entire undiscovered "message system" that controls the self-organizing phenomena encountered in embryological development (which is, of course, the same puzzle Sheldrake's M-field hypothesis attempts to explain). I would like to take this statement further and propose that there is an entire undiscovered set of rules that govern the same self-organizing phenomena in consciousness. In short, as we further decipher the laws that enable poltergeists such as Philip and my own to self-organize as quasi-independent dances, we will find that they are based on the same cybernetic principles responsible for that intricate choreography of thought that we refer to as our minds, that massive example of mind we know as the ecosystem of Earth, the organization of cells in symbiotic colonies of microorganisms, and even perhaps the filamentary structure of the galaxies in the universe.

As Prigogine has pointed out, the fact that even molecules themselves are darting about in an unceasing ballet to find ever more complex patterns of organization should have told us as much—that the universe is alive, right down to its depths, and that the burst of creativity and rudimentary intelligence that is the poltergeist may be less of an anomaly and more of a norm than we think. In short, I would like to suggest that this unending dance of matter indicates that the universe itself is involved in a terrible and glorious chatter, and that little whirlwinds of mind such as the poltergeist are but one more process that is symptomatic of the unending explosion of self-organizing software that is constantly forming, bifurcating, and infinitely exploring itself in the informational backdrop of the cosmos.

If this is the case, two questions immediately arise. The first involves an issue that has been purposefully ignored up to this point in the book. That is, at what level of organization do such software systems become self-aware? For example, is Philip self-aware? And if our personal bias is that he is not (and, hence, that distinct personality, temperament, ability to coherently answer questions, and so on are not criteria indicative of self-awareness), at what level does the dance become self-aware?

Obviously, we humans are self-aware, but if we concede that an organ that may ultimately be the result of a symbiotic colony of bacteria can "think" in ways that seem to transcend the cognitive capabilities of its parts, what rosette of logic can we draw upon to conclude that suprahuman organizations, the biosphere of Earth, or even the entire universe, are not similarly self-aware? This is a particularly discomfiting question to functionalist philosophers such as Dennett, who begrudgingly concedes that the very features that recommend functionalism over other theories of mind also seem to imply that sentience and intentionality may be found in organizations of parts that our common sense tells us are minds "only in the flimsiest metaphorical sense."[38]

The second question is, If poltergeists are another example of a dance of parts and are composed purely of information, how do they manage to move objects around? In other words, how does something that is "no-thing" manage to cross the Rubicon of nonexistence and throw a glass across a room? As we have seen, this is essentially the same as the mind-body problem, or the mystery of how the "nothing" of our thoughts can control the SMA region in our brains, and even perhaps the same as asking how the dance in any of its manifestations manages to be the organizing principle responsible for the design inherent in its parts.

Put more succinctly, how does this ghostly entity we call information, which seems to be something substantially less than either matter or energy, manage to be the prime mover in the universe, and what criteria might we use to determine when an organization of pure information is self-aware of what it is doing? These two questions are the subject of the next chapter, and as we will see, although it may not seem obvious at first glance, they are also, as it turns out, issues that are inextricably related.

# 6

## Schrödinger's Cat Revisited

> Prospero says, "We are such stuff as dreams are made on," and surely he is nearly right. But I sometimes think that dreams are only fragments of that stuff. It is as if the stuff of which we are made were totally transparent and therefore imperceptible and as if the only appearances of which we can be aware are cracks and planes of fracture in that transparent matrix.
>
> — GREGORY BATESON, *Mind and Nature*

IT IS one of the great ironies of our century that as reductionist biologists were slowly trying to purge all mention of consciousness from their understanding of neurophysiological processes, physicists were at the same time uncovering compelling evidence that the mind is not only necessary, but may be integral to our understanding of the physical universe. As was mentioned in the first chapter, the explanation for this conclusion is the fact that even after quanta such as the photon in the double-slit experiment have struck a photographic plate, no amount of scientific ingenuity can determine where they have struck until we actually look at the plate. This fact contains within it not only profound implications about what it means to be a self-aware observer, but tantalizing suggestions about the way that information works in the scheme of our physical universe as well.

No problem better illustrates the strangeness of this apparent connection between the observer and the observed

than a now famous thought experiment known as Schrödinger's Cat. In his imaginary experiment, the Austrian
physicist Erwin Schrödinger pointed out that if one sealed a
cat in a room with a flask of poison gas set to break if a
Geiger counter detected the radioactive decay of an atom
that has a 50 percent chance of decaying, one has no way of
knowing if the cat survived the experiment unless one actually opens the sealed room to observe the result.

In other words, if a physicist tries to mathematically rep-
resent what is going on in the sealed room, the equations
conclude only that both outcomes—both the living cat and
the dead cat—are present in equal proportions. The fuzziness of both the quantum event and the ultimate fate of the
cat are dispelled only when an observer enters the picture
and perceives one of the two mutually incompatible outcomes. Further, a little thought reveals that the dilemma
posed by Schrödinger's experiment does not end with the
cat. For, once an observer has looked into the room, to an
outsider, the observer's knowledge of what they have found
is in the same schizophrenic state as the cat's fate until the
observer has communicated that knowledge to someone
else. In short, the actual fate of the cat seems to exist only in
the ever expanding network of communicating observers.
Put another way, the cat's fate seems to have less to do with
something that exists "out there," and more to do with
something that exists purely in the realm of information.

One question that follows from Schrödinger's hypothetical problem is, If the mathematics seem to imply that before
an observer enters the picture the cat should most properly
be thought of as both alive *and* dead, what happens to one
half of this "superstate" of the cat once the other half has
been perceived by an observer? One school of thought in
physics, known as the Copenhagen Interpretation, believes
that whatever reality or potential for reality the other half
possessed existed only as a statistical reality and never became real. However, an opposing school of thought argues

that there is nothing inherent in the equations of quantum physics that allows us to logically make this assumption. According to this view, the mere fact that our act of observation has allowed only one half of the superstate to manifest does not mean that both are not equally real at some level of reality. To say that one is only a statistical reality is thus arbitrary, an after-the-fact assumption based on our own internal bias, but not on anything inherent in the mathematics of quantum physics.

As a result, this second school of thought, known as the Many Worlds Hypothesis, believes that the other half does not vanish per se, but branches off in a parallel universe that is forever unavailable to our perceptions. In other words, every reaction between a quantum event and an observer, trillions of which are occurring as the light you are reading by hits this page, splits the cosmos into a staggering number of parallel universes in which all of the ghostly states of the quantum are equally real. As might be expected, this view has some rather stupefying implications.

I recently had the pleasure of having a conversation with Alan Guth, a physicist from M.I.T. who is currently best known for his contributions to our theoretical understanding of the origin of the universe (Guth's Inflationary Scenario). After discussing such esoterica as the first unfathomable fractions of a second of the universe's origin and the giant fortress walls of energy that Guth believes may divide one section of the universe from the next, I asked Guth his opinion of the Many Worlds Hypothesis.

After offering the caveat that he did not know how seriously to take the matter, he confessed that if pressed for an answer, he favored the Many Worlds Hypothesis. When I asked him if this meant that there were, at that moment, a multitude of Alan Guths and Michael Talbots carrying on similar conversations in an indefinite number of parallel universes, with obvious reluctance he replied, "Yes. We can't communicate with each other, but we all exist. It's mind-boggling. But it is actually the simplest interpretation of quantum mechanics, or at least I think so. Using the Many Worlds Hypothesis, it seems possible to describe measurements by the same equations that describe any other type of physical process. Obviously, some are of other opinions, and I think most prefer not to talk about it at all. It's one of these metaphysical questions that you can argue about, but nobody can propose an experiment to test between these two different points of view. There don't seem to be any experimentally testable differences, so it becomes just philosophy."

However, whichever interpretation one favors, both schools agree on one point: Quantum events don't really step up into full reality until an observer enters the picture. For those who think that this too is merely a philosophical stance, a further example of quantum strangeness will indicate otherwise. As will be recalled from the first chapter, all quanta possess the dual nature of sometimes behaving like particles and at other times behaving like waves. Intriguingly, unlike the fate of Schrödinger's Cat, which seems to be a random event that is simply triggered by the intrusion of our consciousness, the quantum under other circumstances not only responds to the presence of a conscious observer but actually manifests itself as the observer chooses —as wave or particle.

For example, on the edge of the visible universe is a quasar known to astronomers as 0957 + 561. Quasars are believed to be the exploding centers of distant galaxies, and because they are so far away—some as far away as 13,000 million light years—the light reaching Earth from them actually started its journey billions of years ago when the universe, according to the current wisdom, was but a tenth of its present age. However, the stream of light reaching us from 0957 + 561 does not fall upon Earth directly but has to first pass around an intervening galaxy. The reason that the stream of light coming from the quasar is able to pass around the intervening galaxy at all is because, as Einstein's theory of relativity predicts, the tremendous gravitational field around the galaxy actually bends the space surrounding it, making it function like a gigantic lens.[1]

In a recent article, SUNY cognitive scientist John Gliedman noted that the behavior of a photon when it encounters such a gigantic lens also provides a dramatic illustration of the role an observer plays in helping to create quantum reality. As Gliedman points out, if an experimenter gazes at the light coming from 0957 + 561 with a device designed to see the particlelike aspects of light, measurements of the observed photons will show that, like little particles, each photon either veers to the left or to the right as it encounters the galaxy's gravitational field. However, if the experimenter replaces the device with a mechanism designed to detect the wavelike aspects of light, he will then find that the measured photons received during this operation seem to pass around both sides of the galaxy simultaneously, like ripples flowing around a rock in the middle of a stream.[2]

What is important to note is that the same photon cannot be measured by both devices simultaneously. Thus, by their choice of measurement apparatus, the experimenter either forces a photon to manifest as a particle and pass by one side of the galaxy or forces the photon to manifest as a wave and pass by both sides. In either case the choice of measurement device on the part of the observer irreversibly affects how the photon travels around the galaxy. What makes this connection between the observer and the reality of the photon even more dramatic is that the galaxy it is traveling around is many billions of light years from Earth. In other words, by their choice of measurement apparatus, *the experimenter is altering an event that actually occurred many billions of years in the past.*[3]

What, then, are we to make of this entity we know of as a photon? At the very least, it seems apparent that certain aspects of the photon's reality are not quite real until an observer enters the picture. What is important to note, however, is that the process that takes place between the experimenter and the photon as it passes around the galaxy does not seem to be either energetic or material. No forms of energy or matter that we know of are passing between the experimenter and the photon during this crucial exchange. Whatever interaction is occurring seems to be taking place purely in the realm of information.

Another way of looking at this is that perhaps the two different aspects of the photon's potential reality—its particlelike and wavelike facets—are really like two different channels on a television set. Whether we choose to see the photon going by one or both sides of the galaxy is controlled by a tuning device that exists solely in the software of our thoughts, and when we switch channels we are no more reaching out and affecting the structure of the physical world than we are jostling about the props in a television show when we switch from one channel to the next.

Another important point to remember is that this sensitivity of the photon's reality to certain decisions going on in our heads is not limited to the photon. It is a sensitivity intrinsic to all quantum phenomena. For example, our common sense suggests to us that properties of various quanta such as position, momentum, spin, and so on exist in the same sense as the color of the Mona Lisa's hair or the ebb and flow of the tides, but this is not the case. As the Aspect experiment has now shown, the traits that define any given quantum particle are only blurry potentials waiting for us to make the decisions necessary to lift them up into full existence.

Because of this, in a 1984 address given to the American Physical Society, John Wheeler of the University of Texas suggested that instead of viewing quantum particles as possessing predetermined traits, we might better look at them as being in the same state of existence as the final answer in the surprise version of the game of twenty questions.

For example, imagine that you have been locked in a room while a group of your friends decide on a difficult word for you to guess. When you return, however, you notice that everyone has a grin on their faces. You suspect that some sort of mischief is afoot, but nevertheless you decide to proceed with the game and start asking questions. "Is it an animal?" "No." "Is it a vegetable?" "No." "Is it a mineral?" "Yes." "Is it brown?" "No." "Is it white?" "Yes." As you go on with your questions you notice that each respondent is taking longer and longer to answer. Finally, at the end of the game you are left with one obvious choice. "Is it a cloud?" Your respondent reflects upon this for a moment and then answers, "Yes," and everyone bursts out laughing. Then they explain to you that when you went out of the room, everyone agreed to not agree on a word. Instead, everyone decided they would answer as they pleased with the one proviso that when they answered, they would have to have a word in mind that was compatible with all of the previous answers. Otherwise, if you challenged them, they would lose and you would win. But the final answer, the word cloud, did not exist until you asked your final question.[4]

Wheeler believes that phenomena such as the sensitivity of the photon to our choice of measurement apparatus indicate that at the quantum level the universe is in the same shadowy state as the final answer in the surprise version of the game of twenty questions. What does this mean for the physical universe? Wheeler's answer to this question is as astonishing as it is profound. It is his conclusion that we can no longer view the universe as composed of hardware and existing "out there." Instead, we must begin to view it as composed of "a 'meaning' software" and located, as Wheeler puts it, "who knows where?"[5] In other words, we have to begin to view the universe as ultimately constituted not of matter and energy, but of pure information.

If Wheeler is correct on this point, and I believe that he

is, it is perhaps a conclusion that we should have arrived at long ago. Ever since science embraced Einstein's theory of relativity, physicists have spoken undauntedly of gravity as being nothing more than "curvature" or a "geometric property" of space-time. What is this but another way of saying that it is not composed of a substance or energy, but is just another way that nature encodes information?

It is true that science currently believes that gravity is ultimately associated with its own particular variety of quanta, the so-called graviton and gravitino, neither of which has yet been found. But even if they are, what are quanta composed of? The current wisdom is that quanta, and indeed the essential reality of the universe, are a set of fields, and what are fields composed of? As we have seen, this is not such an easy question to answer.

Many physicists are beginning to believe that, far from being an empty stage, what we know of as a vacuum really possesses quite an elaborate structure. Inspired by work Wheeler did in the 1950s as well as by recent advances, many physicists believe that at its ultramicroscopic level, empty space is really a turbulent and frothy storm of activity. Moreover, it is now accepted by science that in these violent upheavals in the nothingness, new particles are constantly being created and destroyed. Most of these particles have lifetimes so incredibly brief that they are virtually nonexistent, and hence are known as "virtual particles." However, physicists know that virtual particles are more than just abstractions that pop up in their equations because, ghostly and short-lived though these particles may be, they still jostle around the atoms in our own world a bit when they appear, and these effects can be physically measured. Indeed, a growing number of physicists are coming to believe that everything we know as real in the entire universe may ultimately have sprung out of this empty but seething vacuum—perhaps reality is what "no-thing" does when it gets bored.

If quanta are ultimately constituted out of the vacuum—ultimately just structures in the nothingness—what does this mean? What is structured nothingness but just another word for information?

It may turn out to be the grandest irony of all that we are all written on the wind, that something that has always been thought of as being "no-thing" may prove to be the only thing. At the very least, the fact that even in trying to penetrate the most basic secrets of matter we once again run headlong into the omnipresent phantom, that ubiquitous specter information, suggests that perhaps we should give this vacuum in our thinking another look.

## THE ON/OFF UNIVERSE

If information is the ultimate stuff of the universe, the question remains, Given that it seems to lack all substance and energy, how might it contrive to move the sticks and stones of the world around? A suggestion of the answer can be found in the apparent interaction between the observer and the observed. For instance, as was pointed out earlier, the crucial exchange that seems to take place between the experimenter's thoughts and the reality of the photon as it passes by one side of the galaxy or both does not appear to be either a causal or energetic process as we know them. There is no stream of energy or high speed particles reaching out from the experimenter's mind and pushing the photon toward one of its two mutually exclusive destinies. What we have here is an example of a totally new kind of process, a cause and effect relationship that does not take place within the scheme of matter and energy as we know them but takes place completely in the realm of information. John Wheeler calls this process "observer-participancy," and it is suggested that this is one way that the "no-thing" of information exercises its effects in the physical universe.

In confronting this realization, Wheeler asserts that

physics has demonstrated that it is in the early stages of a new scientific revolution, one that will leave in its wake upheavals every bit as radical as those left by relativity and quantum theory.[6] Wheeler calls this new scientific revolution "recognition" or "meaning" physics and believes that it will ultimately allow us to unravel the very foundation of physical law itself.

If the functionalists are right and consciousness should be thought of as pure information, is it any more outlandish to believe that observer-participancy might be responsible for playing the keyboard in the SMA region of the brain than it is to believe that the same "no-thing" of thought can reach billions of years back into the past and affect the course of a photon? In both, it seems that a process that takes place totally within our heads, a decision, somehow seems to cause a real and measurable effect in the physical world.

I believe that observer-participancy will ultimately be found to play some role in the mind-body problem. But if this seems relatively palatable to the open-minded reader, we now arrive at a more difficult question. How, for example, does the same "no-thing" of thought, say the software of a poltergeist, manage to throw a glass across a room? Before embarking on this task I would like to say a word about the phenomenon for which I am about to offer a tentative explanation.

I am aware that psychokinesis, or the ability of mind to have a direct effect upon matter, is by no means accepted as a legitimate phenomenon by the scientific establishment. I believe in psychokinesis because I have experienced it so many times firsthand, but I am fully cognizant of how difficult it must be for those who are entrenched in decades of scientific bias to suspend their prejudice and offer the matter any serious consideration. What I have to say about the matter must be regarded as purely anecdotal, involving my own experiences with a poltergeist, and I offer it only as evidence suggestive that further and adequate scientific inquiry still needs to be made.

However, I do believe that at the core of my own experience with the poltergeist, hitherto undiscovered laws of physics were coming into play. First, I believe that some weight must be given to the consistency and sheer number of events that took place—the number of inexplicable phenomena the poltergeist produced over the years certainly numbered in the hundreds. Second, I believe that the similarity between many of these events and those reported in other poltergeist hauntings throughout history also bears consideration. And third, although many of the phenomena I attribute to the poltergeist might conceivably have ordinary explanations, a few remain so inexplicable that I see no way they can be accounted for without invoking processes not yet recognized by the scientific establishment. For the purposes of this discussion I would like to give examples of two types of manifestation that I feel belong in this category.

For the first example, in the summer of 1976 I was alone in a room in my New York apartment when suddenly a small piece of polished glass came zooming down at a sharp angle from the direction of the ceiling and landed at my feet. There were no open doors or windows in the room, and the area from which the glass originated was a totally featureless expanse of ceiling, with no cracks or fissures in its surface out of which such a piece of glass might have fallen. Further, when I first caught sight of the glass it was still only several inches from the ceiling, and it was only as I watched that it shot down at a 45° angle and covered about half the length of the room to land at my feet. During the course of its existence the poltergeist produced many such "locked room" psychokinetic manifestations.

The second type of phenomena, although rarer than such displays of psychokinesis, presents even more formidable problems for our commonsense notions about physical reality. Those are occurrences in which the poltergeist not only seemed to move objects, but teleport them, causing them to dematerialize in one location and rematerialize in another, some distance away. I have on my desk right at this moment a small piece of polished quartz that I purchased in a rock shop when I was a young boy. I originally added this particular piece of quartz to my rock collection because it has a distinctive shape and looks remarkably like a miniature light bulb. My rock collection remained at home when I went away to college, but one day I noticed that the poltergeist was being exceptionally active, and I asked it if it could teleport objects. At the time, I had no particular object in mind, but the next morning when I awoke, I found my little light bulb of quartz, sitting squarely in the middle of my desk. I was convinced it was the same piece of quartz from my rock collection because of its distinctive shape and coloring, but just to make sure, the next time I went home I checked my rock collection and found that it was indeed missing. Somehow the poltergeist had managed to transport it well over a hundred miles. During the course of its existence the poltergeist produced about a dozen such teleportations.

How might the pure information of the poltergeist move and even dematerialize objects to transport them across such vast distances? If the human mind is able to affect the reality of the photon without actual causal interaction, there is another scheme or frame of reference to reality to which we should be paying more attention. Instead of moving within the world of thing-events, when the human mind interacts with the reality of the photon, it seems that it is operating upon what we might call the "information picture" of the universe as a whole. Or, to employ the metaphor mentioned earlier, the two different and mutually exclusive realities of the photon may be no more objectively real than are different channels on the cosmic television set. This is reminiscent of Bohm's assertion that the apparent interaction between the observer and the observed in quantum physics need not be a causal process, for in an infinitely interconnected universe, consciousness and the thing observed are ultimately no more separate than are different patterns on the same carpet.

What I would like to suggest is that if the software of the mind has the ability to switch between one reality of the photon and the next, making it seem to flip-flop between being on one side of the galaxy or both sides, it may also have the ability to switch between one reality of a small piece of polished glass and the next, making it seem to flip-flop along a successive series of locations as if it were following a specific albeit anomalous trajectory through space. In short, I believe the reason that no mysterious energy has ever been discovered that might account for psychokinetic phenomena is that psychokinesis is not a causal process. It is also a phenomenon that takes place in the information picture of the universe as a whole and is another form of observer-participancy.

How might observer-participancy also account for the ability of the poltergeist to dematerialize objects and teleport them over vast distances? I believe that the answer to this question once again lies in the fact that at its most fundamental level, the ultimate stuff of the universe seems to be pure information. For example, if we do live in a "meaning" universe, and information, not mass or energy, is the ultimate fabric of things, it must be remembered that the question becomes not how does the mass of my little light-bulb-shaped rock crystal dematerialize and travel over a hundred miles, but how does the *information* that is my rock crystal manage to do this? In this age of telecommunications, when large bodies of information are routinely wired every day over vast distances in the twinkling of an eye, it should be obvious that at the very least this is a problem far less intractable.

It should also be remembered that if the phenomenon of teleportation has something to do with observer-participancy and the information picture of the universe as a whole, it is unlikely that the processes involved will be causal as we know them. For example, when an experimenter causes any given photon to choose between going by one side of the galaxy or both sides, "out there" the photon does not suddenly leave one of its apparent locations and shoot pell-mell across the width of the galaxy to arrive at the other. The *information* that is the photon simply ceases to manifest in one of its possible locations and instantaneously materializes in one of its other possible locations instead.

Even disregarding the apparent ability of my poltergeist to teleport objects, the behavior of subatomic particles alone suggests that above and beyond the causal framework of our material reality, at the level of the information picture, the universe processes the information that ultimately manifests as the photons and other subatomic quanta of our world in a highly organized manner. This fact has caused some researchers to suggest that we should be looking more closely at the awesome information-processing abilities of the invisible fabric of space-time itself.

One such researcher is physicist Edward Fredkin of M.I.T. Fredkin believes that it is time we start viewing the universe as a sort of giant computer. Like Wheeler, he also believes that the ultimate substance of the universe is pure information, and this view has caused him to interpret what we perceive as the apparent reality of subatomic particles in a rather startling way.[7]

Fredkin believes that at its most fundamental level the universe functions as if it is composed of a three-dimensional lattice of little on/off switches, like logic units in a giant computer, each one deciding millions of times a second whether to be on or off at the next point in time. In Fredkin's view, a pattern of these switches when they are "on" is what we perceive at our own level of reality as subatomic particles, and when these switches turn "on" and "off" in sequence, that is what we perceive as a particle in motion.[8]

Thus, in Fredkin's universe, subatomic particles—and ultimately the objects they comprise—are no more substantive than the panoramic images generated by the card-holding sections of stadium crowds when they create giant portraits of Lenin, Mao Tse-tung, or a University of Southern California Trojan. What we perceive as an electron is like an image in these cards. It is merely a pattern of information, and an electron in motion is simply that pattern in motion.[9]

Whether or not Fredkin's theory is correct in all its details, something very much like it seems to be going on in the world of subatomic particles. For example, as we saw in Chapter 1, the quantum-tunneling effect seems quite bizarre to us if we imagine electrons as hard little objects. But if they are just patterns of information, it may be no more difficult for the cosmic computer to make them vanish in one location and reappear in another than it would be for the card-holding section of a stadium audience to make a portrait of Lenin vanish from one end of their network of cards and instantaneously reappear at the other.

Similarly, it is difficult for us to imagine that objects could possess the properties of both a particle and a wave, but if we view these dual aspects of a subatomic particle as just different patterns of information, it becomes easier for us to comprehend how they might be intermingled. It may be that at the quantum level the patterns of information that might ultimately manifest as either a particle or a wave are still superimposed, like two different pages from a book projected onto a single screen.

David Bohm has argued that because even the concept of trajectory breaks down at the quantum level, and science has not yet arrived at an adequate description of how one moment in the life of a quantum particle is connected to the next to result in something even vaguely resembling flow or movement, we must cast a suspicious eye toward trajectory and movement at our own level of existence. Bohm feels that part of our problem is trying to comprehend how seemingly discontinuous quantum events can add up to create a sense of flow and movement, and that we still view quantum particles (and perhaps even pieces of polished glass) as inherently separate from the background of reality through which they seem to be flying.

Bohm suggests that if the universe is infinitely interconnected at some deeper level of reality, instead of viewing a particle as an object traveling through empty space, it might be better to view it, at any given point in its trajectory, as something that unfolds out of this deeper level of reality, only to *enfold* back into it again, and then unfold out at the next point in its trajectory, and so on.[10] What Bohm is suggesting here is not so different from Fredkin's view of the universe, that the notion of movement being a series of unfoldings and enfoldings is similar to the notion of movement being a series of switches turning on and then going off again, or the idea of an image unfolding out of a sea of cards in a stadium audience, only to enfold back again, and so on. In such an infinitely interconnected universe, it is implied once again that the ultimate stuff of reality is information.

All of this suggests that the ability of the poltergeist to dematerialize objects is really no great feat. When my own poltergeist dematerialized the bulb-shaped rock crystal and transported it over a hundred miles, it was not transporting an object but only a pattern of information. No real movement of the rock crystal actually took place. The pattern of information that is the rock crystal simply ceased to exist in one location and instantaneously began to exist in another; "wired," as it were, through the infinite interconnectedness of the information picture by the software of mind in a process little different from the transaction that allows the mind to instantaneously cause a photon to appear on one side of the galaxy or both sides, or allows a computer to instantly cause a cursor to skip from the top of the computer screen to the bottom.

Indeed, if the universe is a "meaning" universe, if process and not substance is the final arbiter of all those transactions that eventually manifest to us as reality, we must conclude that we humans arc all only a step above the nether region of the "virtual" particles. The only difference is that whereas a virtual particle appears and then quickly vanishes, the flicker of our own existence resulting from the millions of switches comprising our body at any given point in time is just a little more prolonged.

If we knew how to control the mechanism responsible for this process, we too could simply interrupt the switching on and off a little, could cease to exist in one flicker of our apparent continuity and reappear in another, anywhere in the computer screen of the universe that we chose. As tantalizing as the prospect of teleporting ourselves and other objects in such a manner is, given that the software of our minds already seems to be infinitely interconnected to the information picture, such a teleportation process may even turn out to be one of the cruder modes of transportation available to us in a "meaning" universe.

## TRAVELING IN THE INFORMATION PICTURE

During the past ten years, two laser physicists named Harold Puthoff and Russell Targ of the Stanford Research Institute (SRI) in California have uncovered another way they believe the mind interacts with the level of quantum interconnectedness—what we've been calling the information picture. In a series of articles they have detailed their work on a remarkable and hitherto unvalidated human capacity they call "remote viewing." What they have found is that many individuals are able to accurately describe what's going on in distant locations even when all normal modes of perception are blocked, almost as if they are able to use the information level of the universe as a medium through which the pure information of their thoughts can travel.

The setup of Puthoff and Targ's experiment was as follows. First, a series of target locations were secretly chosen and sealed in envelopes by the director of the Information Science and Engineering Division at SRI. The envelopes were then arranged in random order and locked in the division director's safe. Next, a test subject and an experimenter with no prior knowledge of the target locations were closeted in a special double-walled, copper-lined room designed to prevent all possibility of radio contact. After the subject and experimenter were sequestered, a team of experimenters was then given one of the envelopes at random and instructed to go to the location specified in the envelope. After one-half hour of travel time had elapsed, allowing the team time to reach the location, the experimenter remaining behind asked the subject to describe his impressions into a tape recorder and make drawings to illustrate these impressions.

In one such test a retired police commissioner who claimed that he had often used his remote viewing ability in his police work gave the following description of the location he thought two experimenters were visiting: "What I'm looking at is a little boat jetty or little boat dock along the bay. It is in a direction about like that from here (points in the correct direction). Yeah, I see the little boats, some motor launches, some little sailing ships, sails all furled, some with the masts stepped and others are up." He added, "Funny thing—this flashed in—kinda looks like a Chinese or Japanese pagoda effect. It's a definite feeling of Oriental architecture that seems to be fairly adjacent to where they are."[11]

As Puthoff and Targ state in a later write-up of the experiment, "He [the commissioner] was describing quite accurately what in reality is a restaurant located on the dock. His voice on the tape continued, correctly describing the granite slabs leading down to the water's edge, indicating our location as being four miles northeast of SRI, and so on.''[12] The performance was not a one-time thing. Time and again Puthoff and Targ discovered that the commissioner as well as numerous other test subjects were able to describe distant locations, accurately, occasionally even mentioning some by name.

To date, Puthoff and Targ have published their results in scientific publications ranging from *Nature* to the *Proceedings of the Institute of Electrical and Electronics Engineers*, and over a dozen similar studies performed by other research groups have duplicated their results.[13] Although much about remote viewing remains unknown, several intriguing facts have come to light. To begin, the phenomenon does not seem limited by distance. Secondly, since electrical shielding does not appear to degrade the quality or accuracy of perception, it appears that the signaling processes involved are probably not electromagnetic in nature. Equally intriguing, Puthoff and Targ find that remote viewing is not limited to individuals already professing psychic abilities, such as the police commissioner. Indeed, some of their best subjects turned out to be individuals with little or no previous experience in the paranormal. Thus, Puthoff and Targ conclude "that remote viewing is probably a latent and widely distributed perceptual ability."[14]

Lest anyone jump to the conclusion that the test subject simply is tuning in telepathically to what the experimenter is seeing, Puthoff and Targ offer several other findings that challenge even this hypothesis. For example, Puthoff and Targ found that test subjects often described targeted locations, not from the perspective of the experimenter's eyes, but from a vantage point high overhead, as if they were zooming in from an altitude of several thousand feet. In one test involving the police commissioner the targeted location was a local marshland nature reserve. The subject attempted to describe the location: "I get this image of crosshairs—

looking at crosshairs. We're getting closer. It's more like an intersection. I get the feeling of a botanical area, with cross-walks, very geometrically laid out." As it later turned out, the nature reserve was filled with crosswalks that were very geometrically laid out, but the fact that they resembled cross-hairs at their points of intersection did not immediately occur to the experimenter, for this was an aspect of the crosswalks that became visible only in an aerial photograph of the nature reserve.[15]

These aspects of remote viewing are reminiscent of my lucid dream of the lost de Maupassant book, and in their 1977 book *Mind-Reach*, Puthoff and Targ acknowledge the similarities between remote viewing and out-of-the-body experiences. Because remote viewing does not seem to rely on any known energetic processes, they also confess their belief that it must have something to do with the level of quantum interconnectedness. If there is any question that the processes responsible for remote viewing take place at the information level of the universe as opposed to our own matter-and-energy-oriented level of thing-events, one last fact about this remarkable human capacity will put these murmurings aside.

As is obvious, at our own seemingly objective level of existence, causality reigns supreme, and transactions involving matter and energy are strictly bound by the one-way flow of time. As we have also seen, at the information level of the universe these restrictions break down. Curious as to whether remote viewing was limited by the constraints of time, Puthoff and Targ tried an unusual variation on their normal method of experimentation. Instead of having the test subject try to describe the targeted location after it had been chosen, they decided to see if the subject could describe the location *before* it had been chosen.

In one such study an experimenter was given nine sealed envelopes, each containing a different location unknown to the test subject, and told to drive around aimlessly. While the experimenter drove around aimlessly, the subject was asked to try to visualize where the experimenter would be in half an hour. The subject answered, "I got a quick flash of a black pointed area, like a, like a head of an arrow. He walks into it. It's like a triangle that he walks into." The subject then described a sound that she asserted seemed to follow the person's passage into this black triangle: "It's a rhythmic kind of squeak, like a rusty pump, or a not-well-oiled piston. Just a very rhythmic squeaking."[16]

Half an hour later, randomly choosing a sealed envelope to open, the experimenter traveled to the location described therein. Completely unaware of what the subject had related earlier, he found himself at a small park in which there was a black triangle in the form of a child's swing. Knowing that he was supposed to stay at the location for a little while, to pass the time he went into the black triangle, sat down, and started to swing in the rusty swing, oblivious that its rhythmic squeak had been heard by the subject *half an hour before the actual and randomly chosen event.*[17]

As startling and remarkable as it may seem, Puthoff and Targ's work reveals that when the consciousness operates at the level of the information picture, not only is it no longer bound by the confines of space or distance, but it is also no longer restricted by the one-way flow of time. The SRI experiment, as well as numerous others conducted there, reveal that beyond the shadow of a doubt the human biological organism possesses the ability to leap into the future, to actually tap into information about future events and process that information in the present.

This may seem strange to us, for it has been ingrained in us to believe that we are frozen in the one-way river of time, but the ability of an organism to pull information from the future and process it in the present may be a far more natural state of affairs than we have previously realized. Biologists have always assumed that the mechanisms of evolution are similarly confined by the one-way flow of time, but there remain numerous anomalies that suggest that the biological world is also able to occasionally overcome certain evolutionary imperatives by entering the future. Because this idea has always been viewed as manifestly impossible by the scientific establishment, only a few researchers have even been courageous enough to admit that there are unsolved evolutionary puzzles. One such researcher was the eminent naturalist Loren Eiseley. Toward the end of his life Eiseley confessed, "I am simply baffled. I know these creatures have been shaped in the cellars of time. It is the method that troubles me."[18]

In his book *Lifetide*, Lyall Watson notes that one such unexplained puzzle can be found in an insect known as *Laternaria servillei*, a three- to four-inch-long relative of the cicada that lives in the water plants along the shores of the Amazon River. What is unusual about this planthopper is that mother nature has painted on its back the perfect likeness of a small alligator, accurate in every detail, right up to its white and grinning bas-relief teeth and small white marks in exactly the right places to simulate the glint of watchful reptilian eyes. The purpose is, of course, to scare the daylights out of the predators that might normally feed upon the planthopper, but the mystery is, How did this insect acquire this masterful bit of *trompe l'oeil*?

As Watson points out, if the image had evolved slowly over time, before it looked so forbodingly like a baby alligator, then while it was still an amorphous blotch of white on the insect's back it would not have provided an evolutionary advantage at all, but would have attracted the attention of predators and thus imperiled the planthopper. The only alternative is to believe that the image blossomed into being fully formed, and this presents a problem to the normal evolutionary view of things.[19]

Watson notes that the living world is filled with such anomalies—designs and relationships so complex that it seems that they could not have arisen by sheer chance, but had to have sprung into being fully architected. Another example is the tarantula wasp. When it is ready to lay its eggs, the wasp finds a tarantula spider and stings it. Because the wasp knows precisely where to sting the tarantula, the spider does not die but is permanently paralyzed. The wasp then lays its egg on the living and immobile spider and seals the spider, egg and all, in a hole in the ground. It does this so that when the wasp larva hatches it has a store of living food to devour as it matures safely in its dark enclosure. But the miracle does not end there. Somehow the wasp larva knows precisely how to consume the living spider, saving the vital organs until last, so that the spider does not die and decompose until the wasp larva has reached maturity. Only then does the wasp break forth from its burrow to start the cycle anew.

The wonder is that at some point in the distant past the very first tarantula wasp to attempt this procedure had to perform it correctly the very first time. Had the first wasp to discover the technique stung the spider at any other spot than the correct one, it would have either killed the spider, rendering it useless as a food source, or merely injured it, causing it to turn and kill the wasp in retaliation. In other words, the wasp had to sting the spider at precisely the right point in the spider's nervous system that would result in paralysis, otherwise there would be no young wasp to inherit the talent. Similarly, the very first wasp larva so engendered would have to have known precisely how to go about eating the spider to ensure keeping it alive, otherwise the spider would have died and decomposed, resulting in the death of the larva. In either case it just does not seem possible that such uncanny abilities could have arisen spontaneously and by accident.[20]

Such mysteries are not limited to the insect world, and even Darwin himself admitted the difficulty of accounting for many of the complex behaviors and forms of living organisms. In *The Origin of Species* he stated, "To suppose that the eye with all its inimitable contrivances for adjusting the focus to different distances, for admitting different amounts of light, and for the correction of spherical and chromatic aberration, could have been formed by natural selection, seems, I freely confess, absurd in the highest degree."[21]

If natural selection is not the explanation, how did the tarantula wasp acquire its remarkable talents? One possible answer is that, just as human beings are able to occasionally gain information from the future, perhaps, at some point in the distant past, the very first wasp that dared to combat a spider encountered in that confrontation an evolutionary imperative that allowed it to pull a little information back from the future. Perhaps, in that life-or-death struggle, the wasp retrieved from its own species' future just enough information about the spider's anatomy to enable it to make a new evolutionary advance.

If this is correct it may be that in conjunction with the Darwinian mechanisms of evolution, there is another scheme at work; that on occasion, when some unknown and perhaps especially critical bifurcation point is reached, it is part of the operating procedure of nature to transcend the strictly causal framework of Darwinian evolution and allow an organism to self-organize certain aspects of its behavior and/or design across the boundaries of time. This is, of course, roughly analogous to what Sheldrake says a species does with the M-fields of its past, but the point is that perhaps the ability of the subject in Puthoff and Targ's experiment to hear the squeak of a swing half an hour before the event actually took place is not so "supernatural" at all. Perhaps occasionally tuning into and operating at the level of the information picture is simply nature's backup system, as normal and organic a process as when certain bifurcation points, such as the injury or death of a loved one, allow us to tune into our own apparent backup systems of precognition and clairvoyance.

Such a process might also explain the enigma of evolution itself. According to the current and prevailing biological view, all evolutionary advances are accidental and drawn from the ocean of the random. And yet, in spite of the undeniable element of chance and statistical variation in the living world, nature still seems to possess at its core an unerring drive toward greater complexity. Where does the information inherent in this complexity come from? According to the current view we can only say that it comes from nowhere, that nature, by dint of some unfathomable alchemy, perpetually draws more and more information into its fabric and that this information appears out of nothing. Is it that much more incredible to propose that nature perpetually draws its ever increasing stores of information not from the void but from the future, or from the information backdrop of the universe as a whole?

Indeed, perhaps the fact that the dance can so often transcend its parts—that a symbiotic colony of bacteria can be drawn toward a design quite beyond the reckoning of its individual components, and even the fact that order can blossom suddenly out of chaos—are all ultimately the result of similar sorts of informational flux. Perhaps the reason the sudden appearance of such new patterns of order seems so startling and magical to us is that the ultimate source of such new surges of information is not the causal scheme of things, but the information level of the universe as a whole. If this is the case, if the cosmic backdrop of information is the backup system that self-organizing entities can tap when they are overwhelmed by especially critical bifurcation points, the information picture of the universe may not simply be just a level of infinite interconnectedness, but a reservoir of contingency plans and designs. Perhaps this is what David Bohm was getting at all along when he said that there is tremendous order enfolded in the glycerine, that at its implicate level the universe seems capable of pouring forth such a diversity and richness of forms that nature itself must be considered purposive and intentional.

Whether or not these phenomena turn out to be similar examples of informational flux, the fact remains that Wheeler's "meaning" universe still seems to be looming large on the scientific horizon. Challenging evidence is being offered from a number of different directions that information, not mass or energy, is the ultimate fabric of the cosmos. The level at which matter and energy cease to be the currency of transaction, and information becomes the coin of the realm, seems to form another level of reality, another plane of existence, as it were. The laws of physics that govern the seemingly objective world also break down, cause and effect as we know them no longer apply, and even the boundaries of time evaporate. From this one is led to ask, If the ordinary laws of physics no longer operate at the level of the information picture, do any laws operate at all? Is the level of information governed by its own, presently unknown but separate body of laws?

Fredkin for one believes so. Because he believes that information is not purely a creation of the human mind but was there all the time waiting for the technology that would allow us to empirically study it, he also believes that in time the universal properties of information will also be discovered. For example, Fredkin proposes that there may be a conservation of information law on the level of the information picture, just as there is a conservation of matter and energy law at our own level of existence.[22]

At the very least, Fredkin suggests that there are unknown rules that allow the cosmic computer to operate, which is why at our own level of existence, the "graphics displays" created by this universal computer—such as electrons, protons, subatomic particles in motion, and so on—seem to follow such universal laws.[23] For those who find it difficult to believe that the universe is run by a universal computer, it has been pointed out before that conventional physics already has within its skein of understanding a similar sort of *deus ex machina*. As physicist and Nobel laureate Richard Feynman has stated, the important thing about physical law is not "how clever we are to have found it out, but . . . how clever nature is to pay attention to it."[24] Similarly, as Robert Wright, the senior editor of *The Sciences* put it in a recent article on Fredkin's work, "The universe is permeated by a kind of intelligence, however you look at it, and it is scarcely more ludicrous to declare, as Fredkin does, that 'the universe is run by a computer' than to suggest, as physicists implicitly do, that 'the universe is run by the ministry of differential equations.'"[25]

If Fredkin is right and unraveling the laws that allow the universal computer at the information level to operate also allow us to unravel not how but *why* the laws of physics operate, we arrive at the fulfillment of precisely what Wheeler predicts the accomplishment of "meaning physics" will be. Wheeler has called this slowly coalescing scientific revolution Era III physics (Era I being the physics of Galileo and Kepler, or the cataloguing of motion with no explanation of motion; Era II being the mechanics of Newton through the quantum theory, or the cataloguing of law that explained change, but with no explanation of law). Era III physics is the culmination, or deciphering, of physical law itself.

Like Fredkin, Wheeler also recognizes perhaps that the devaluation of the terms *matter* and *energy* in favor of the "no-thing" of information, will not come easily. As he states, "How can anyone even dream of abandoning for the foundation of existence a physics hardware located 'out there' and putting in its stead a 'meaning' software . . . ? And how can the hard-won structure of hard science be moved over, solid as ever, onto this new and other-worldly foundation? Yet, despite all difficulties, and they are great, that must be the task and achievement of the coming Era III of physics."[26]

How and where might we go about probing the secrets of such a meaning universe? First, it is clear that the processes that govern the universe at the level of the information picture once again lie in those regions beyond the quantum. It is suggested that if and when our technology allows us to penetrate even more ultramicroscopic levels of existence, we will begin perhaps to gain a toehold in the shadowy realm of the cosmic computer.

However, the profoundest message inherent in the evidence we have that this information level exists, from the photon traveling around the galaxy in the previous example to Puthoff and Targ's research on remote viewing, is that the true gateway to its discovery perhaps lies through the mind of a conscious observer. If this is the case, and given that we have come full circle—from the mind trying to discover the secrets of matter and back to finding out that those secrets have something to do with the mind—at the very least we should begin to question, What defines a conscious observer? This brings us once again to the matter of precisely what criteria we might call upon to define when a dance of parts, any dance of parts, from the human brain to other, should be classified as a conscious observer.

## When Does the Dance Become Self-Aware?

Until his dying day Einstein was extremely disturbed by the entire notion that the mind might have something to do with the ultimate reality of the world. His discomfort became especially pronounced when he took this view to its logical conclusion and pointed out that if a human observer could alter a quantum event through the mere act of observation, there was no reason to exclude the possibility of a nonhuman observer doing the same thing. As he stated doubtfully at a seminar just shortly before his death, "If a person, such as a mouse, looks at the world, does *that* change the state of the world?"[27]

Wheeler, who embraces many of the implications of quantum theory that Einstein found most abhorrent, takes a more liberal view. He quite matter-of-factly accepts that in the quantum universe, nothing exists until it is observed. As he states, "It may be that we could not have anything that would be meaningful existence in default of some community of (intelligent biological or mechanical) observers."[28]

As for what he means by intelligence, Wheeler asserts that his definition of the term is synonymous with its usage in AI research. By this he admits the possibility of an intelligent robot also qualifying as an observer. However, curiously—and contrary to the thinking of at least some AI researchers—he denounces the use of the term *consciousness*, but his motive for this rebuff appears mainly to divorce himself from any endorsement of the idea of consciousness existing as a nonmaterial something.[29] In his writings, Wheeler clearly implies that he defines intelligence as "meaning-sensitive," and as for how he defines "meaning," he invokes the same definition employed by the philosopher Dagfinn Føllesdal, that meaning is "the joint product of all the evidence that is available to those who communicate."[30] However, in the end, one is unsure whether or not Wheeler believes a mouse changes the world when it looks at it.

To define an observer merely as meaning-sensitive also leaves a particularly intriguing question unanswered. For example, in 1983 researchers at Penn State published the startling discovery that trees communicate. It seems that trees under attack by insects or animals release an unidentified chemical into the air as a stress signal, which causes nearby trees to step up their own chemical defense systems. Further, the Penn State researchers found that the nearby trees stepped up production of their chemical defenses proportionate to the duration and intensity of the attack experienced by the trees sending the original signal.[31]

No less amazing was another disclosure in 1983 that plants have memories. Researchers at the Université de Clermont, France, found that when they pricked young marigolds with needles the plants would "remember" for periods of up to thirteen days the direction from which they had received the pinpricks and would grow in different directions. The French research group found that the plants' memories seemed to be dependent on ion supply, thereby suggesting that although plants do not have a nervous system, the basic cellular mechanism of memory and information retrieval is still present.[32] Thus, according to Føllesdal's definition, it seems that we must regard plants as meaning-sensitive, but do they also qualify as observers in the quantum mechanical sense?

Another definition for what it means to be a conscious observer has been offered by numerous researchers, namely that a conscious observer must be able to make a simulation of the world so complex that it can include itself within that simulation. However, even here our normal prejudices about what it means to be self-aware are in for a bit of a shock. In the spring of 1983, the Smithsonian Institution held a symposium on animal intelligence at which a number of researchers reported even more challenging evidence that we are wrong in our bias, our Ptolemaic Conceit, that we are the only conscious species inhabiting this planet.

For instance, Princeton ethologist and internationally renowned expert on honeybee behavior, James L. Gould, revealed one finding of his own that even he found difficult to accept. Gould confessed the standard wisdom is that most signs of animal intelligence are the result of innate or "prewired" behavior patterns. However, in a recent experiment he found discomforting evidence to the contrary even in the lowly honeybee. In the test, Gould's purpose was to observe the ways bees locate new food sources. To accomplish this task Gould provided honeybees with desirable food sources,

and after they became accustomed to feeding at the stations
he set up for them, he moved the food sources by a factor of
1.25 the distance of the previous move. What Gould found
was that after a few such moves the honeybees no longer
had to search for the new location, but anticipated Gould's
behavior so accurately that he found the bees circling the
new location before he had even arrived and waiting for
their food.[33]

At the very least, the honeybees were able to construct
quite a complex simulation of reality in their tiny (less than
4/10,000 of an ounce) minds and deduce from past experience where in that simulation Gould was going to place the
food next. When asked if he could explain how the bees
accomplished such a remarkable feat, Gould replied, "I
can't. I wish they'd never done it!"[34]

Indeed, if one associates true intelligence with behavior
that seems less prewired and more unique, and if one defines true observer-participants in the universe as those entities that display the meaning-sensitive ability to both
process and communicate information in a unique way, as
we have seen, this intelligence extends all the way down to
the quantum level of matter. Inherent in the unpredictability
of every quantum particle is the fact that it seems to be
processing information in a unique way. Inherent in the
way that electrons seem to make decisions about whether
or not to penetrate a barrier in the quantum-tunneling effect
is the fact that they seem capable of processing information.
And inherent in the seeming interconnectedness of subatomic particles revealed by the Aspect experiment is the
fact that quite a complex meaning-sensitive web of communication seems to take place among particles.

As is now well known, this has caused some physicists
to conclude that even subatomic particles are, in their own
vestigial way, conscious. Physicist Freeman Dyson of the
Institute for Advanced Study at Princeton recently said:

I cannot help thinking that our awareness of our own brains has something to do with the process which we call "observation" in atomic physics. That is to say, I think our consciousness is not just a passive epiphenomenon carried along by the chemical events in our brains, but is an active agent forcing the molecular complexes to make choices between one quantum state and another. In other words, mind is already inherent in every electron, and the processes of human consciousness differ only in degree but not in kind from the processes of choice between quantum states which we call "chance" when they are made by electrons.[35]

Throughout his life, Gregory Bateson steadfastly rejected this view, claiming that "atomies" could not possess "mental striving," for by his own definition, a mind cannot be just one part, but must be composed of many parts. However, it must be pointed out that perhaps the greatest lesson to be gleaned from the Aspect experiment in particular and quantum physics in general is that atomies are not atomies at all, but part of an indivisible web in which it is no longer meaningful to speak of things such as electrons as separate parts abstracted from the fabric of the whole. In light of this fact, the foundation on which Bateson bases his argument collapses.

Just as the boundaries between living and nonliving matter dissolve, and those qualities that we define as intrinsic to life are present in varying degrees through the panorama of natural phenomena in the universe, the same is true of consciousness. Meaning-sensitive intelligence is present in human beings and honeybees and also in subatomic particles, and although we may be able to set up vague conceptual gestalts and parameters for measuring the degree of self-awareness in any given self-organizing system, such yardsticks are useful as job-specific tools, but are in the long run illusory.

Put another way, in a universe that is infinitely interconnected, although self-awareness may functionally be viewed as if it is localized in the various whirlpools and eddies that self-organize out of the apparent atomies of matter and energy in the universe, such localizations are ultimately as meaningless as asking where the signal responsible for the image on a television screen is most powerfully focused in the actual picture.

In a meaning universe, what we perceive as a degree of consciousness in any given self-organizing entity is at least partially a measure of that entity's ability to tune into the cosmic backdrop of information. In other words, what we perceive as degrees of self-awareness in ourselves and other self-organizing systems is partly a measure of the transactions we (or they) are carrying on within the information picture of the universe as a whole at any given point in time. It follows that given the proper bifurcation point (the proper influx of energy and/or information), it is possible for any self-organizing system, no matter how seemingly primitive, to suddenly and unexpectedly display an entirely new degree of self-awareness or attribute of mind.

This ultimate nonlocality of consciousness in the universe is perhaps why it is so difficult to pinpoint precisely where consciousness is located in our biological brains. For if the *what* of consciousness is that it is pure information, in a meaning universe the *where* of consciousness becomes alternatively *no*where and *every*where. In a universe that is infinitely interconnected, consciousness can be anywhere it wants to be—in the dance of neurons in our brains, in a disembodied poltergeist, drifting lazily over a lost library book in one's own backyard, or zooming down over a nature reserve outside of Stanford, California. As we learn more about the information picture of the universe, our ability to tap into it with our minds will improve, and when we set out to explore the cosmos we will not do so in metal ships, but in constructs of pure information.

In the meantime, if there is any lingering vestige of prejudice that observer-participancy is limited to *Homo sapiens*, one last example will cut it asunder. In the early 1970s, physicist Helmut Schmidt of Duke University decided to see if he could uncover evidence of psychokinetic ability among animals. To do this, Schmidt linked a binary random-number generator to a heat lamp and placed the setup in a garden shed outside his home. He also arranged that the random-number generator would turn the heat lamp on and off at completely random intervals. As if it were hooked to a flipping coin, Schmidt knew that the laws of probability then dictated that the lamp should be on approximately half the time and off approximately half the time. In a trial run, and while the shed was empty, the lamp did just that, showing no tendency to stay on or off with any unusual frequency. Then Schmidt placed a cat in the shed during cold weather and once again contrived that the apparatus would keep a record of how often the lamp was on and how often it was off. To his surprise, Schmidt found that the presence of the cat made all the difference in the world, and the lamp stayed on far longer than would be expected by chance alone.[36]

Obviously the cat is meaning-sensitive enough to know that it is better to be warm than to be cold, but it is doubtful it knew that its presence was altering its reality a bit. Thus, it seems unlikely that the awareness of the transaction that resulted in the cat's having a more advantageous environment necessarily resided in the thought of the cat. To ask how self-aware the cat is of its situation is less meaningful than to ask how self-aware the information picture of the universe is as a whole. This question, and the answer that various researchers have recently offered, is one of the subjects of the next chapter.

# 7

# Mathematical Evidence of the Existence of God

> One can envisage creatures whose capabilities are
> so great we could not distinguish their activities
> from nature itself. This hierarchy would involve a
> supreme being possessing the greatest power and
> intelligence. Such a being would fulfil many of the
> traditional requirements of God.
>
> —PAUL DAVIES, *God and the New Physics*

FOR THE MOMENT put aside the question of precisely what
type of organism constitutes an observer-participant. What
is truly important is that accepting the primacy of observer-
participancy brings with it another challenging implication.
Since without observers it must be accepted that the universe would not exist, it must be assumed that the universe
had built into it the potential for containing observers.

In the past decade quite a number of amazing coinci
dences in the laws of physics, coincidences that imply the
universe was designed for the purpose of creating conscious
entities capable of observing and understanding it, have
come under scientific scrutiny, and currently there is an active debate about what these amazing coincidences mean.
Some scientists believe that the human race, through billions of acts of observer-participancy traveling back through
time, has actually had a major role in creating both the
universe and the laws of physics. Others feel that the exis-

tence of such coincidences provides us with mathematical evidence for the existence of God.

It is a remarkable thing, and little known among the general public, that science is seriously discussing such extraordinarily mystical issues at all. At a 1983 symposium on the constants of physics held by the Royal Society, one of the subjects that figured prominently on the agenda was a notion that goes by the innocuous name of the "Anthropic Principle."[1] Taken from the Greek term *anthropos,* meaning "man" in its current usage, the Anthropic Principle purports that it is man's observations of the universe that have helped mold what we perceive as the laws of physics.

The Anthropic Principle was first coined in the mid-1970s by Cambridge astrophysicist Brandon Carter, and Carter's inspirations are the incredible numerical coincidences that seem to have come together in nature to allow the formation of stars. For example, as is now widely known, the life of a star is a constant struggle between the forces of gravity which strive to cause the star to collapse in upon itself, and the forces of electromagnetism which work against gravity and struggle to keep the star from collapsing.

Carter observed that the balance of power between these two forces is so incredibly fine-tuned that it is quite difficult to conceive of this balance being the result of coincidence alone. For instance, if as the universe were forming, the strength of the force of gravitation had varied by as little as a mere one part in 10,000,000,000,000,000,000,000,-000,000,000,000,000 (1 part in $10^{40}$), this delicate balance would have been destroyed and stars such as our Sun would never have formed.[2] Since life as we know it is contingent on the existence of stars such as the Sun, it follows that the existence of the human race also rests on this precarious balance. In other words, the existence of life on Earth hangs on a thread far slenderer than that which held the sword of Damocles.

Freeman Dyson has pointed out another such coincidence. In the nucleus of an atom, protons and neutrons are held together by a powerful cohesive force known as the strong nuclear force. Dyson has noted that if as the universe were forming this force had been only slightly weaker than it is, protons and neutrons would not be able to hold together and atoms as we know them would never have formed. Conversely, if the force had been minutely stronger, it would then have been possible for protons to stick together, and long ago all of the free protons in the universe would have been mopped up like so much glue, preventing the formation of atoms and stars and people.[3]

The list of such coincidences goes on and on. Sir Fred Hoyle, along with California Institute of Technology astrophysicist William A. Fowler, has pointed out that oxygen and carbon, two of the most important elements on which life on Earth is based, are designed almost perfectly so that they will be produced in the interiors of stars in equal amounts. If this were not the case, and one or the other predominated in the universe, the development of life would once again have been precluded.[4]

What does it all mean? A conclusion more scientists are reaching is that the activities of observers at all points in time are constantly self-organizing and streaming back through time, guiding the development of the universe throughout its history.[5]

This is a staggering thought. Can it be that when astronomers turn their telescopes to the heavens they are not discovering evidence of the Big Bang, but are helping to create it? Do these coincidences in the way the universe is put together exist because we humans have reached back through time and placed them there? Incredibly, science has brought us to the point where we can seriously ponder such questions.

Needless to say, not all physicists accept such matters. One criticism of the Anthropic Principle is that it is an entirely *post hoc* (or after the fact) theory and has not yet been used to predict any undiscovered feature of the universe. Another criticism is that the Anthropic Principle lacks the physical foundation necessary to make any theory scientifically acceptable.[6]

However, this last criticism has been at least partially answered in a now famous article by Cambridge astrophysicists Bernard Carr and Martin Rees published in *Nature*. Carr and Rees wrote, "Such a foundation may already exist in the . . . 'many worlds' interpretation of quantum mechanics." In other words, if all possible universes exist, it must be assumed that many universes exist in which the laws of physics did not come together in precisely the right way to allow for the development of life as we know it. In some the force of gravity did vary just enough so that stars collapsed early in their evolution and flooded the universe with deadly X rays. Others remained stillborn with nothing even this interesting happening in them. In this view, in only a very few universes—ours included—did the laws of physics come together in exactly the right orchestration of events to allow the universe to become "aware of itself."[7]

Not all proponents of the Anthropic Principle find this a suitable explanation. Princeton physicist Robert Dicke, himself one of the early supporters of the Anthropic Principle, argues that if these other universes remain forever unknowable, it is senseless to even talk about them.[8] Ironically, Wheeler, who was one of the original founders of the Many Worlds Hypothesis, has also rejected the notion of an infinite ensemble of universes on the grounds that it carries with it too much metaphysical baggage.[9] Wheeler now feels that it is only proper to speak of one universe; it's just that the presence of observers in that single universe results in the finely-tuned laws of physics.

Perhaps the most important criticism leveled against the Anthropic Principle, however, is that it bespeaks a Ptolemaic Conceit. Carr and Rees point out in their article that the notion that the human race alone is responsible for the fine-tuning of the visible universe is an "unduly anthropocentric concept" of what it means to be an observer. Carr and Rees concede that the Anthropic Principle may never aspire to being much more than a philosophical curiosity. They go on to add that the number of amazing coincidences that continue to be uncovered in the laws of physics is still astounding. In their final remarks, Carr and Rees conclude that even if all such coincidences are explained, it is still remarkable that over and over the relationships dictated by the laws of physics are the same as those that are propitious for life.

## THE MYSTERIOUS OCEAN

There is an old, true saying that a fish cannot see the water in which it swims. We humans are swimming in a most extraordinary ocean, a sea of events so astounding, and yet so much a part of our everyday reality, that it is difficult to take a step back and perceive their full wonder. Although the coincidences that inspired the Anthropic Principle may jump out at us at the most obvious junctures of design in our seamless universe, there is another mystery in our midst even more profound—that we understand the universe at all.

Because our universe is part of the water in which we ourselves swim, its uncanny regularities and interweavings of order are not readily apparent to us. We take it for granted that every morning the sun will rise; when we strike a match, it will light up; when it rains, it probably will not rain molten lead down upon our heads; and that throughout our daily existence the panorama of the laws of physics will remain comfortingly stable. And yet, in a universe in which all possible frameworks of reality might have resulted, it is possible that quite a different universe might have developed through time.

It is conceivable that as sentient beings we might have found ourselves born into a universe in which the laws of physics were not so regular, an Alice-in-Wonderland existence in which random processes completely prevailed and the laws of nature had gone so berserk that day-to-day existence was a haphazard hodgepodge of events more like an LSD trip than a regular and flowing passage from day to night.[10]

Most often physicists, like the rest of us, tend to accept this miracle without comment, and go about their business thinking primarily of their work, and perhaps what they are goind to have for dinner that evening. But every once in a while something happens that stirs them in their slumber, and reminds them once again that they are indeed swimmers in a mysterious ocean.

For example, in a recent article Paul Davies described the work of a number of different physicists all puzzling over the thought problem of what might happen if a box full of heat radiation were lowered on a rope toward the surface of a black hole. The notion was first pondered in the early 1970s by Jacob Bekenstein when he was still a graduate student at Princeton. In vastly simplified terms, what bothered Bekenstein was that if such a box were emptied of its contents near the surface of a black hole, and then pulled away from the hole once again, it would return with a mysterious surplus of energy. Since we live in a universe in which nature keeps very close track of her energy deficits and credits, and quantities of energy simply do not "pop out" of nowhere, Bekenstein was deeply troubled by his finding.

The solution to the problem came in 1974, when Stephen Hawking of the University of Cambridge announced a spectacular discovery. By combining the mathematics of quantum theory with the physics of black holes, Hawking discovered that black holes are cloaked in a veil of heat radiation now known as Hawking radiation. Employing Hawking's finding, William Unruh of the University of British Columbia and Robert Wald of the University of Chicago found the solution to Bekenstein's mystery. To contain a quantity of heat radiation, the walls of Bekenstein's box must be made of a highly reflective material. However, the same property that served to keep heat radiation in the box would also keep the Hawking radiation out. As a result, as the box is lowered it displaces some of the radiation enshrouding the hole, creating an upthrust on the box in the same way the displacement of water keeps a boat afloat. As Davies commented, although Archimedes "would probably turn in his grave," it was his celebrated principle of buoyancy at work.[11] When the box is opened to empty its contents, it will attract some of the Hawking radiation that shrouds the hole. This is the source of Bekenstein's mysterious surplus of energy.

As Davies pointed out, although no one is suggesting that such an experiment could ever actually be performed, what is astounding about Bekenstein's problem is that it reveals that even under the most exotic of circumstances, nature is meticulous about the way her laws of physics dovetail. And although here and there a physicist may temporarily forget a law or two, nature does not, and like a master storyteller, she always remembers where every character belongs. This miracle is the very reason that inspired Fredkin to assert that the universe functions as if it were a giant computer. All too often we do not give nature its awesome due, that the regularity of our lives is indeed in the benevolent hands of an invisible ministry of differential equations.

The creative principle responsible for this fact does not matter, for the amount of organization inherent in this flawless drama is mind boggling. And even more amazing, the laws of physics are not only consistent, regular, and seamlessly interlocked; they are comprehensible.

This thought has been pointed out before, but it is a state of affairs so familiar to us that we often do not grasp its full wonder. The fact that we can understand the universe is most often referred to by scientists in terms of the beauty of a theory. Time and again we are persuaded that an idea or an equation is correct because of its elegance. No scientist working today can deny that aesthetics, something that is purely a product of the inward reality of our consciousness, also provides us with the map for discovering the workings of the outward reality of the universe. But why is this so? Why is it that theories born of a quest for beauty turn out also to be true? Or as Yale biophysicist Harold Morowitz has put it, Why is it, when we work through Newton's second law of motion for the first time, we get "the feeling of a return to some primordial knowledge"?[12]

Nowhere does this feeling of a return to some primordial knowledge become more apparent than in the world of mathematics. As Einstein wrote in 1921, "Here arises a puzzle that has disturbed scientists of all periods. How is it possible that mathematics, a product of human thought that is independent of experience, fits so excellently the objects of physical reality? Can human reason without experience discover by pure thinking the properties of real things?"[13]

In a now famous paper entitled "The Unreasonable Effectiveness of Mathematics in the Natural Sciences," written in the late 1950s, Nobel Prize–winning physicist Eugene Wigner asked the same question. After examining several examples of the applications of very abstract mathematics to specific problems in physics, Wigner concluded that the structure of mathematics and the structure of the physical universe are indeed disturbingly similar. Wigner capped off his paper with a quote from the late philosopher and physicist Charles Peirce "that there is some secret here which remains to be discovered."[14]

Is mathematics unreasonably effective in describing what's out there? To many physicists this is a question so disturbing that they prefer to leave it unanswered. Some counter by suggesting that the uncanny effectiveness of mathematics is an illusion, born out of the fact that the world of mathematics is so huge that we have only picked the ones that are effective.

There can be no doubt that this is true to a certain extent. Mathematician Morris Kline of the Courant Institute pointed out in his recent book, *Mathematics: The Loss of Certainty*, that in the twentieth century a tremendous amount of mathematics has been generated which has not yet found any practical applicability in the world of science. However, certain mathematical models still prove jarringly effective in describing the physical world, and the fact that mathematical models have been generated which do not yet have practical applicability does not demonstrate that their applicability will never be found.

Take, for example, the case of University of Chicago mathematician and astrophysicist Subrahayam Chandrasekhar. For twelve hours a day, seven days a week, Chandrasekhar sits at his desk and relentlessly searches for mathematical beauty in the landscape of his thoughts. On one such cerebral journey in the 1960s he caught a glimpse of that beauty in a geometric mathematical entity known as an ellipsoid. Discovering that other mathematicians had also worked on these tangerine-shaped figures but had left the sum total of human knowledge about them fragmentary and sketchy, Chandrasekhar set out to explore their full wonder.

During this time, other scientists accused him of wasting his energies and asked why he was bothering to spend so much time studying an abstraction that did not exist in the real universe. Ignoring them, and perhaps invigorated by the feeling that he too was unraveling a piece of primordial knowledge, Chandrasekhar persevered, even publishing an entire book on the subject. It wasn't until twenty years later, after scientists began to study more intently the different shapes of galaxies, that it was discovered that Mother Nature does indeed use the ellipsoid in her machinations, and scientists now routinely use Chandrasekhar's book to understand such things as what holds the Milky Way together as it spins.[15]

Science and mathematics abound with such occurrences. In the nineteenth century, mathematician Bernard Riemann discovered an entirely new system of geometry, but no one knew that it was any more than just a mathematical curiosity until Einstein used it in his general relativity theory of gravity. In the 1950s, physicists Chen Ning Yang and Robert Mills became enraptured with an esoteric group of mathematical entities that they subsequently called gauge fields. Yang and Mills were drawn to gauge fields because there was an inscrutable "rightness" about them, but no one knew that these splendidly elegant mathematical entities had any practical application until the 1970s. Now it is believed that virtually all of the forces of nature may be describable in terms of gauge fields.

Why is this so? Why, while sitting at a desk, is it possible for Chandrasekhar to discover the universe in his head? Why, while exploring constructs of pure information in the landscape of our thoughts, do we encounter these resonances of familiarity? Why, in the words of the late physicist Sir Arthur Eddington, have we discovered a strange footprint on the shores of the unknown, and when we reconstruct the creature responsible for that footprint, we find that it is our own? More than just the coincidences mentioned earlier connect us with the cosmos. When we look out at the stars, we see the same laws, the same tremendous organizations that also govern thought.

Nor must we accept that the fact that we find a bit of ourselves in the laws of physics is due simply to our inability to view the universe from anything other than a human perspective. We have reached a point where the interconnectedness we perceive between ourselves and the universe cannot be explained as mere Ptolemaic Conceits. We humans are connected to the universe, to the distant past of the Creation, and no doubt the remote future as well, in a way that goes far beyond unavoidable human bias.

As we have seen, one explanation for this interconnectedness is the Anthropic Principle. However, in light of the criticisms of the Anthropic Principle, some researchers have recently pointed out that there is another explanation that should be given serious consideration by science. That is, the reason there are similarities between the way we think and the way the universe is constructed is that some intelligence beyond us has placed them there, has created us both.

## GOD AS AN EXPLANATORY PRINCIPLE IN SCIENCE

In his 1983 book *God and the New Physics,* Paul Davies argues that science has reached a point where it is hard to resist the impression that the present structure of our universe, apparently so sensitive to minor alterations, has been rather carefully thought out. Davies concludes that one possible explanation is that the existence of these coincidences might be attributed to God. Davies asks, "[Is it any easier] to believe in a cosmic designer than in the multiplicity of universes necessary for the weak Anthropic Principle to work?" After conceding that since neither hypothesis can be tested in a strictly scientific sense, Davies maintains that the presence and vast number of these coincidences still remains "the most compelling evidence for an element of cosmic design."[16]

Davies goes on in his book to entertain other possibilities. For example, after acknowledging that consciousness and intelligence are software, he argues that taken to its logical conclusion, this point of view leads to another possible explanation. In a universe in which mind is software, it is possible to imagine an overall gestalt of consciousness, a supermind, existing since creation, encompassing all the fundamental fields of nature, and taking upon itself the task of ordering the laws of physics.

Davies states, "This would not be a God who created everything by supernatural means, but a directing, controlling, universal mind pervading the cosmos and operating the laws of nature to achieve some specific purpose. We could describe this state of affairs by saying that nature is a product of its own technology, and that the universe *is* a mind: a self-observing as well as self-organizing system. Our own minds could then be viewed as localized 'islands' of consciousness in a sea of mind, an idea reminiscent of the Oriental conception of mysticism. . . ."[17] In such a self-organized hierarchy of mind, one can envisage creatures whose capabilities are so great that we could not distinguish their activities from nature itself.

This view has also been recently expressed by another eminent scientist. In his 1984 book *The Intelligent Universe*, Sir Fred Hoyle boldly asserts that scientific evidence indicates that the universe is governed by some sort of interlocking hierarchy of intelligences. Hoyle bases his conclusion not only on the felicitous and anthropic coincidences that have cropped up in our current understanding of the laws of physics, but also on an occurrence that Hoyle finds equally improbable—that the creation of biological life on Earth was the result of a purely random sequence of events.

The currently accepted wisdom in science is that life began in the primordial soup of Earth's ancient seas and was the result of a completely random orchestration of events. The justification for this view is that given enough time and enough accidental permutations of chemicals in such a primordial broth, it is possible that any complexity might have arisen. Similarly, and for a number of years now, adherents to this view have also pointed out that given enough time, a large work force of monkeys with an equally large number of typewriters could sooner or later come up with all the works of Shakespeare.

The problem with this view, according to Hoyle, is not that it is theoretically unsound, but that it is realistically impractical. In a recent article, mathematician David Osselton chided his fellow mathematicians for ever popularizing the issue of the monkeys and the typewriters in the first place. As Osselton points out, the basic mathematics behind the notion that given enough time a group of monkeys would eventually manage to type the works of Shakespeare may be simple and sound, but the sheer enormity of such a task makes it meaningless as an explanatory principle. According to Osselton's calculations, it would take a million million monkeys roughly a million million years to type out only the name of William Shakespeare. And to obtain a paltry two lines from one of Shakespeare's plays would require $10^{150}$ strokes on a simplified fifty-character typewriter, or billions of billions of time more than the number of atoms in the whole universe. Osselton concludes, "The idea that in the fullness of time random events will ineluctably come up with the right combination is less potent than has been commonly supposed."[18]

Hoyle invokes the same argument: It is known that a living cell has a chain of amino acids, of which there are twenty different kinds. The function of these amino acids is in turn dependent upon 1,000 to 2,000 highly specialized enzymes. Hoyle postulates that for an enzyme to work by the amino acid chain, assuming its correct configuration in space, at least twenty to thirty key amino acids must be "right." According to Hoyle's calculations, the probability of a thousand different enzymes coming together in just the right way over the course of Earth's several billion years of history to form one living cell is a staggering $10^{40,000}$ to 1.

Francis Crick, who shared a Nobel Prize for his work on the structure of DNA, likewise concluded, "An honest man, armed with all the knowledge available to us now, could only state that in some sense, the origin of life appears at the moment to be almost a miracle, so many are the conditions which would have had to have been satisfied to get it going."[19]

If biological life did not originate by accident, how did it first arise? Hoyle believes that life did not originate on Earth, but was seeded here by infection from space, and that the cosmos is pregnant with living organic material whose true origins are lost many billions of years in the universe's misty past. Further, on noting that random processes tend to destroy order, and intelligence shows itself most effectively in arranging things and producing order out of chaos, Hoyle concludes that the complexity of life indicates that the universe itself is intelligent, and that it is this intelligence, or hierarchy of intelligences, that first wrought the order in matter that resulted in living things.

Not content with just these extraordinary assertions, Hoyle believes that the hierarchy of intelligence in the universe has probably undertaken many great experiments. For example, he asserts that it is unlikely that the organic life that he believes now pervades the cosmos was always carbon-based. He suggests that at some time in the distant past, when the fine-tunings that allowed carbon-based life to exist in our present universe were different, another form of life, perhaps silicon-based, prevailed. Hoyle believes that carbon-based life came about when the software of intelligence that manifested in this silicon-based hardware, our remote interstellar ancestors, perceived that the laws of physics were slowly shifting, and that this ancient hierarchy of intelligence quite literally designed the hardware or DNA necessary to give the next great wave of life in the cosmos its present carbon-based form. Hoyle believes that the activities of this hierarchy of intelligence, like the activities of Davies' hypothesized hierarchy of intelligence, are currently indistinguishable from the activities of nature itself.

Whether or not Hoyle is right about life being carbon-based throughout the universe, or whatever the ultimate molecular form the hardware of life takes, the significant thing to note in his work is the assertion that the quintessence of both intelligence and life is software, or pure information. Further, Hoyle believes that for even our remote interstellar ancestors to have self-organized out of the hurly-burly of matter whatever form their hardware took would have required the existence of an organizing principle, what Hoyle believes to be an overall gestalt of intelligence or pure information that exists beyond time. Indeed, Hoyle believes that the reason this overall gestalt of intelligence has become so advanced is that it self-organizes beyond time; that it reaches out from all points in the remote and infinite future back to all points in the infinite past, quite literally lifting itself up by its own bootstraps, feeding itself in the past the very information that will allow it to become so unfathomably intelligent in the remote future.

Currently, evolutionary theorists have come to recognize that the evolution of life on Earth is not a gradual process taking place in discrete steps but is most often an abrupt and sudden process, with new designs and advances in organisms appearing quite suddenly. Hoyle suggests that perhaps the mechanisms responsible for this new view of evolution, known as "punctuated equilibria," are the result of processes similar to the backward time flow that has allowed the overall gestalt of intelligence in the universe to self-organize. This is, of course, the same sort of beyond-time informational flux suggested in the previous chapter as being responsible for such biological anomalies as the miniature alligator on the back of the Amazonian planthopper.

Because of this similarity of processes between the universal intelligence and biological life on Earth, Hoyle concludes that perhaps there is a connecting chain of intelligence, extending downward from the intelligence of the universe as a whole to the intelligence of those hierarchies of software whose activities are indistinguishable from nature "by a series of further links to humans upon the earth." [20] As further indication that this hierarchal and interpenetrating chain of intelligence exists, Hoyle offers one last bit of evidence.

Hoyle notes the fact that there seems to be a universal religious impulse or spiritual drive in humanity that has, in this era of intellectual enlightenment, come to be viewed as an archaic remnant, a whispering of something primitive and unsophisticated. However, says Hoyle, perhaps this restlessness, this unquenchable urge that has driven thousands of martyrs to their deaths to support their various belief systems, that has inspired the human race for thousands of years to build extraordinary monuments reaching heavenward toward various anthropomorphized gods—perhaps this religious impulse is just our awareness of our connectedness to this hierarchy of intelligence. Perhaps, when stripped of its many fanciful adornments, our religious impulse is little more than the simple encoded message within each of us: "You are derived from something "out there". . . . Seek it, and you will find much more than you expect." [21]

## A PROBLEM OF LANGUAGE

The age-old message of the mystics is that the macrocosm is the microcosm. But does the evidence in this chapter suggest that the universe is intelligent, that the concept of an overall gestalt of consciousness or supermind should be installed as an explanatory principle in science?

The evidence presented in this chapter suggests that the universe is indeed pregnant with intelligence, and there is a usefulness in acknowledging this fact, but I do not believe that the value of recognizing the existence of a supermind lies in its use as an explanatory principle. To say that the apparent existence of this supermind explains anything per se is to make the same error as believing that the existence of the laws of physics ultimately explains anything. Another great era of discovery still lies ahead of us, one in which we will begin to unravel not only the secrets of physical law, but the further complexities and processes underlying the existence of this universal intelligence as well. Put another way, acknowledging the apparent existence of a universal intelligence at work in the cosmos does not suggest we abandon the empirical tools of science, nor that we should allow the trappings of any given religious belief system to be mapped over by science. All this merely signals that the next great era of human discovery is about to begin.

Acknowledging the existence of a universal intelligence involves as much a transition of language as it does a transition of human understanding. It is a transition that is already taking place in science. For example, is it really any different to recognize that the universe functions like a giant computer than to recognize that it functions like a giant mind? Similarly, is there any fundamental difference in saying that the universe is pervaded by highly organized information than in saying that it is pervaded by consciousness? If consciousness and life are ultimately only measures of information, are the terms not interchangeable?

This being the case, it might be argued, why bother making any transition in language at all? If Western science was so uncomfortable with the notion of the existence of a non-material consciousness and could only begin to seriously explore the mysteries of self-awareness by substituting another term in its stead—by calling it software or pure information—why should we make the transition back to more humanistic and anthropomorhic terms?

One reason is that such a transition might help to restore meaning to our existence. In spite of all of its positive attributes, the purely reductionist and mechanistic approach has tended to make us view the universe as a giant and accidental machine in which we humans are merely random "glitches." But we are more than just machines. The lesson of the new physics is that there are prodigious murmurings of intelligence in all things, and by opting for the term *mind* over *computer*, and recognizing that we are part of the living fabric of the cosmos, it is possible that we will go far toward reinstating some of the meaning we now so sorely lack. As Davies puts it, "The far-reaching philosophical implications of the new physics should not be ignored by the physics community. . . . The new physics has room for a meaning to existence," it is just that the language to describe this ultimate reality is not yet to be found "in the familiar world of daily discourse." [22]

Such a transition might also underscore our connectedness with all things. It is clear that many of the world's current problems are due to divisiveness, selfishness, and fragmentation. The fact that the new physics contains within it powerful metaphors of self-transformation and social transformation should also not be ignored. Effecting such a shift in language and consciously emphasizing that we humans and the universe we inhabit are all part of a living, intelligent, and infinitely interconnected fabric might be a good first step toward trying to heal these ills.

Another advantage that such a transition of language might bring with it is that it might make it easier for us to recognize the directions of investigation necessary to make the discoveries that will eventually allow us to explore those worlds beyond the quantum. For example, if we choose to deny that there is an intelligence at work in things and follow the current trend in science to acknowledge that the tremendous order we find throughout the universe is "explainable" merely in terms of being self-organizing activity, this is tantamount to recognizing only that the universe is, in a way, our own "termite nest," and if we view its flawless architecture as simply a wonderful gift that cannot be further understood, we will remain at our own level of "termitehood."

However, if we view it as an expression of intelligence— a value-laden term that by definition already brings with it a suggestion of further thought, motivation, purpose, and creative expression—we will more easily recognize that to say something is the result of self-organizing activity is ultimately no more of an explanation than to say it is the work of a deity. This is a hurdle necessary if we are to ever enter Wheeler's Era III of physics and begin to decipher the foundation of physical law—a domain of processes, which as we have seen, seems to lie at the level of the information picture. We must, at the very least, acknowledge in our language that there are processes waiting to be discovered if we are to ever begin to penetrate those worlds beyond the quantum.

Hand in hand with this last point is the fact that such a transition of language may also allow us to begin to see qualities and relationships that we might otherwise have overlooked. For example, the fact that information is the quintessence of both consciousness and living processes in general might lead us to suspect that it may also possess other organic qualities as yet undiscovered.

In Western science this organic aspect of information has occasionally been perceived by mathematicians, although little understood for what it really means. The Soviet mathematician I. R. Shafarevitch seems to brush up against this realization when he compares the abstract entities encountered in the pure information landscape of mathematics to living organisms, noting only that the processes responsible for their formation seem less self-aware and more instinctive, or more akin, as Shafarevitch puts it, "to the growth of crystals."[23]

Mathematician Stanislaw Ulam expresses a similar sentiment when he observes that the seemingly endless number and variety of abstract concepts encountered in the pure information plane of mathematics is strikingly reminiscent of "the prodigiality of nature." As Ulam notes, in the abstract plane of mathematics one is witnessing the same explosive creativity that "produces a million species of different insects."[24]

An even more intriguingly organic aspect of information has been pointed out by Oxford zoologist Richard Dawkins. Dawkins observes that when life first appeared on Earth, one of the first talents that it had to master in order to embark on the path of biological evolution was the ability to make copies of itself, or "self-replicate." Citing the evidence of the fossil record, Dawkins concludes that the first replicators on Earth were living molecules. At some point in evolution these replicating molecules discovered another powerful survival strategy, the ability to enclose themselves within protein walls. Equipped with such armor, Earth's early replicators enjoyed greater protection from the elements and from each other, and Dawkins believes it is from these first primitive cells that the panoply of life on Earth evolved.

But where are these replicators today? Dawkins states, "They did not die out, for they are past masters of the survival arts. But do not look for them floating loose in the sea; they gave up that cavalier freedom long ago. Now they swarm in huge colonies, safe inside gigantic lumbering robots, sealed off from the outside world, communicating with it by tortuous indirect routes, manipulating it by remote control. They are in you and me; they created us, body and mind; and their preservation is the ultimate rationale for our existence. They have come a long way, those replicators. Now they go by the name of genes, and we are their survival machines."[25] In short, Dawkins believes that in a sense we are only a taxi service for our genes. We die, but the gene does not. It simply moves from organism to organism down through the generations, always striving to maintain its own immortality, but caring not at all about the survival of any single one of its organismic taxis.

However, Dawkins believes that genes are not the only replicators on the planet. In his book *The Selfish Gene*, he posits that a new type of replicator has recently emerged on Earth. It is still in its infancy, still drifting clumsily about in its own primordial soup, but already it is achieving evolutionary change at a rate that leaves the old gene panting far behind. As Dawkins sees it, the new replicators are "ideas" or "units of pure information," and the soup is the soup of human culture. Because ideas replicate themselves by being communicated from one person's mind to the next, Dawkins calls the new replicators "memes," after the Greek word "mimeme," meaning *imitation*.

Dawkins' colleague N. K. Humphrey states that like genes before them, "memes should be regarded as living structures, not just metaphorically but technically. When you plant a fertile meme in my mind you literally parasitize my brain, turning it into a vehicle for the meme's propagation in just the way that a virus may parasitize the genetic mechanism of a host cell. And this isn't just a way of talking —the meme for 'belief in life after death' is actually realized physically, millions of times over, as a structure in the nervous systems of individual men the world over."[26] This is, of course, not to necessarily suggest that ideas are self-aware of what they are doing. It is only to point out that the way information manifests in both the landscape of mathematics as well as in the landscape of human thought in general is perhaps a shadowy reflection of the way that intelligence operates in the universe at large.

The question of whether genes or even memes are self-aware of what they are doing remains as pregnant an issue as the question of whether subatomic particles possess rudimentary flickers of consciousness. All that seems obvious is that in the infinity of dances of information in this cosmos, certainly others besides ourselves have become self-aware. To assume otherwise would be the pinnacle of Ptolemaic Conceit. There are probably qualities that resemble self-awareness in the hierarchies of intelligence inherent in the formation of the galaxies, the DNA chain, and the laws of physics, which resemble a great chain of being. Again, these would be self-awarenesses so beyond us that their activity would be indistinguishable from nature itself. There may be nothing in this universe that does not possess some degree of self-awareness.

To the argument, if there are hosts of sentient beings throughout the universe, why haven't they landed on the White House lawn, I offer one humble suggestion. Given that as a community of intelligent beings becomes increasingly self-aware it might be expected that such a meaning-sensitive network would also engage in ever increasing acts of observer-participancy, it may be that each community increasingly self-organizes its own channel or frequency out of the information bank of the universal intelligence. In other words, just as we seem to be choosing only one channel in the information picture of the universe when we choose whether any given photon goes by one side of the galaxy or by both sides, perhaps unavailable to our current perceptions are other communities of intelligent beings choosing other channels. In fact, perhaps the reason we perceive so many anthropic coincidences in the universe is that the human race is not perceiving the universe in its totality, but only in one of its many information channels.

This, of course, brings us back to the Many Worlds Hypothesis, and the question becomes, Are all communities of sentient beings forever isolated from one another in their separate universes? I suspect they are not, although if two completely alien communities of intelligence encounter one another, the anthropic prejudices of each would probably impede the ability of one to perceive the information channel of the other. For example, it is said that when Magellan went ashore on Tierra del Fuego, the natives could see him and the rowboats he had come ashore in, but were completely incapable of perceiving his ship anchored just a short distance out in the harbor. It is suggested that Magellan should be thankful that at least his own anthropic prejudices and the Tierra del Fuegoans' anthropic prejudices were similar enough that at least they could perceive him. Had they been of two truly distinct communities of intelligence, they might have been more rigidly sealed in their respective reality bubbles and unable to perceive each other at all.

We speculate here only about communities of sentient beings still inhabiting the material universe as we know it. It may be that in unraveling the secrets of the information picture we may ultimately fulfill the age-old spiritual promise of loosing this mortal coil entirely and become creatures composed totally of pure information. Indeed, perhaps that is the destiny of all meaning-sensitive networks of intelligence. If this is the case, it is conceivable that our stage of operation would no longer be the physical universe at all but another realm entirely. In the spirit of pure speculation, we will explore this prospect a little further in the next chapter.

# 8

# Virtual Particles and Virtual Beings

> You think that objects exist independently of you,
> not realizing that they are instead the manifesta-
> tions of your own psychological and psychic
> selves. . . . The fact is that each of you create your
> own physical reality: and en masse, you create both
> the glories and the terrors that exist within your
> earthly experience. Until you realize that you are
> the creators, you will refuse to accept this responsi-
> bility. Nor can you blame a devil for the world's
> misfortunes. You have grown sophisticated enough
> to realize that the Devil is a projection of your own
> psyche, but you have not grown wise enough to
> learn how to use your creativity constructively.
>
> — SETH, *Seth Speaks*

IN THE AUTUMN OF 1963 a young writer named Jane Roberts
was sitting at her desk in her home in Elmira, New York,
when suddenly her mind flooded with thoughts and aware-
nesses that were not entirely her own. She later wrote, "A
fantastic avalanche of radical, new ideas burst into my head
with tremendous force. I was . . . connected to some incredible source of energy. . . . It was as if the physical world were
really tissue-paper thin, hiding infinite dimensions of reality,
and I was suddenly flung through the tissue-paper with a
huge ripping sound."[1]

During the course of this experience, Roberts' hand
scribbled furiously, and when she returned to normal consciousness she discovered that she had written a batch of

notes on ideas unfamiliar to her, all gathered under the intriguing title *The Physical Universe as Idea Construction*. Shortly thereafter, Roberts, who had never experienced any psychic phenomena before, started lapsing into trances, and an entity who called himself Seth and who claimed to be a personality "no longer focused in physical reality," began to speak through her. Perceiving the obvious quality of the information, Roberts had her husband, Robert F. Butts, take careful notes of everything Seth said. Claiming his purpose was to teach, from that time until Roberts' death in 1984, Seth dicated over 6,000 typewritten pages on such topics as the nature of physical matter, human and animal intelligence, time and reality, the interaction between consciousness and reality, other probable universes, and much more.

Psychologists who had conversations with Seth quickly recognized that they were in the presence of a "massive intellect." Eugene Barnard of North Carolina State University, who had a long philosophical discussion with Seth, writes, "The best summary description I can give you of that evening is that it was for me a delightful conversation with a personality or intelligence or what have you, whose wit, intellect, and reservoir of knowledge far exceeded my own. . . . In any sense in which a psychologist of the Western scientific tradition would understand the phrase, I do not believe that Jane Roberts and Seth are the same person, or the same personality, or different facets of the same personality. . . ."[2]

Regardless of the ultimate nature of the Seth phenomenon (a communication from a being no longer focused in physical reality or a product of Roberts' unconscious mind), the mere magnitude, coherence, and intellectual quality of what Seth had to say indicate that he was a phenomenon deserving of further scientific study.

As Roberts saw it, because Seth alleged that the borders between all consciousnesses are ultimately indistinct and bleed into one another (a view not unlike Bohm's notion of

all consciousness being connected at the implicate level of
reality), she did not see why the two disparate views—that
Seth was either a dramatization of the unconscious or an
independent personality—are necessarily contradictory.
After expressing her own conviction that the term *unconscious* is "a poor one, barely hinting at an actual open
psychic system, with deep intertwining roots uniting all
kinds of consciousness . . . ," Roberts conceded that even if
Seth was purely a product of her own unconscious, it is
something to be marveled at that the volume and quality of
his work never taxed or impinged upon the output of her
own more conscious writing endeavors. After finishing her
weekly output of Seth material—the content of which she
was largely unaware of until she herself read her husband's
transcripts of the sessions—she would then go to work on
any one of her own numerous book projects.

Roberts concluded, "Looked at merely as an example of
unconscious production . . ." the body of Seth's work
"clearly shows that organization, discrimination, and reasoning are certainly not qualities of the conscious mind
alone, and demonstrates the range and activity of which the
inner self is capable."[3] However, Roberts confided that her
own opinion was that Seth was indeed an organized consciousness existing in an aspect of reality other than our
own, and although the filter of her unconscious no doubt
and unavoidably colored what Seth had to say, the information he had to impart was as much news to her as it was
to her many fascinated readers.

Although basically agreeing with Roberts' opinion on
the matter, Seth was more assertive about his independent
status. He stated, "You may, if you wish, call me a subcon-
scious production. I do not particularly enjoy such a desig-
nation, since it is not true." Over the course of his
communications Seth offered other arguments for his separateness from Roberts. As he pointed out in a trance session
Roberts allowed a college psychology class to witness:

My memories are not the memories of a young woman. My mind is not a young woman's mind. I have been used to many occupations, and Ruburt [the name Seth preferred to call Roberts] has no memory of them. I am not a father image of Ruburt's, nor am I the male figure that lurks in the back of the female mind. Nor does our friend Ruburt have homosexual tendencies. . . . I was not artificially "brought to birth" through hypnosis. There was no artificial tampering of personality characteristics here. There was no hysteria. Ruburt allows me to use the nervous system under highly controlled conditions. I am not given a blanket permission to take over when I please, nor would I desire such an arrangement. I have other things to do.[4]

As for what he was, Seth was equally candid: "I am simply an energy personality essence, no longer focused in physical matter."[5] Seth asserted that part of the data bank on which he drew the information that comprised his self-organized identity was once human (indeed, Seth claimed to have lived many lives as a human), but he also claimed that much of his identity was not human but was a symbiotic organization of awareness drawn from a variety of sources of intelligence.

Most intriguing of all was his description of where he lived. As Seth explained, his arena of awareness was no longer in the realm of matter or energy as we know it, but was a level of existence somewhat removed from ours, one in which information or pure thought constituted the major structure. Expressing a view to what we've been calling the information picture of reality, Seth noted that the environment in which he manifested was not bound by the same laws of space and time that govern our own, and hence was also nonlinear and allowed organizations of consciousness such as Seth to "focus upon and react to an infinite variety of simultaneous events." He further added that there were many personalities like himself inhabiting his particular aspect of existence, and stated, "We realize that we form our own reality, and therefore do so with considerable joy and creative abandon. In my environment you would be highly disoriented, for it would seem to you as if it lacked coherency."[6]

As stated, Seth asserted that his purpose in manifesting in Roberts was to teach. "What I will tell you has been told before throughout the centuries, and given again when it was forgotten. I hope to clarify many points that have been distorted through the years. And I offer my original interpretation of others, for no knowledge exists in a vacuum, and all information must be interpreted and colored by the personality who holds it and passes it on. Therefore I describe reality as I know it, and my experience in many layers and dimensions."[7]

Seth also explained that the human race is not the only community of intelligence for which he performs this function, and because some of them are very different from our own he often had to draw upon different aspects of his own mega-personality to make himself understandable to them. He explained, "All systems of reality are not physically oriented, you see, and some are entirely unacquainted with physical form. Nor is sex, as you understand it, natural to them. Therefore I would not communicate as a male personality who has lived many physical existences, though this is a legitimate and valid portion of my identity."[8]

Seth also warned that a sort of observer-participancy is unavoidable when he communicated with different communities of sentient beings, and in this regard, asserted that part of his reason for choosing Roberts as the vehicle for his communications was that he felt she would color what he had to say the least with the filter of her own prejudices. Interestingly, he also chidingly asserted that many other multidimensional personalities who have communicated through humans throughout history have been far less meticulous than he about the clarity of their transmitting channels.

Most astounding of all is what Seth had to say about the

true nature of reality as we perceive it. First and foremost, he noted that through a process tantamount to Wheeler's billions upon billions of acts of observer-participancy, we have created our own reality. We do not realize it because, as Seth put it, at a certain stage in every species' evolution, this process is embedded so deeply in the species' unconscious that they are completely unaware that they are the creators of what Seth calls their own "camouflage system of reality."

We ourselves inhabit what Seth calls a "matter concentrated" system of reality, and as long as we remain ignorant of the fact that consciousness is the sole creator of the universe as we perceive it, we will remain seemingly entrapped in a plane of existence in which cause and effect seem to be the primary operants. However, as we slowly learn that our own focuses of conscious are like tuning systems and that there are many reality pictures that we can tune into, we will begin to more fully understand that thought is the ultimate substance of everything. Foreshadowing the idea that information is the basic constituent of everything, Seth noted that physical objects are quite literally like words or symbols in another medium of expression. He stated, "You create them as surely as you create words. I do not mean that you create them with your hands alone, or through manufacture. I mean that objects are natural by-products of the evolution of your species, even as words are."[9]

Seth asserted that when we finally come to grips with this fact, as a natural step in our evolution we will begin to perceive other veneers to reality, levels of existence in which the pure information of thought reigns supreme, and in which cause and effect as we presently perceive them, as well as space and time as we know them, are no longer of primary importance.

We humans will discover, Seth asserted, that our unconscious minds are already deeply connected to these levels, but for the most part, our conscious minds presently edit out our awareness of them because our intellectual capabilities are not yet equipped to handle the volume of data encompassed by this interconnectedness. For example, in his own apparent endorsement of the Many Worlds Hypothesis, Seth alleged that every earthly event does indeed play itself out in all probable states; that each quantum particle as well as every human being and historical event does indeed have an infinite series of probabilistic counterparts, and that being infinitely interconnected with these parallel universes, we are as multidimensional as he is, and the focus of our awareness simply is just not yet tuned in to this fact.

However, as Seth explained, "In greater terms, it is impossible to separate one physical event from the probable events, for these are all dimensions of one action. It is basically impossible to separate the 'you' that you know from the probable you's of which you are unaware. . . . There are always inner pathways, however, leading between probable events; since all of them are manifestations of an act in its becoming. . . . The physical brain alone cannot pick up these connections with any great success. The mind, which is the inner counterpart of the brain, can at times perceive the far greater dimensions of any given event through a burst of sudden intuition or comprehension that cannot be adequately described on a verbal level."[10]

This, of course, leads to a rather mind-numbing view of the universe. Seth stated, "The rockbed reality is the one in which the perceiver is focused. From that standpoint all others would seem peripheral. Taking that for granted, however, any given reality system will be surrounded by its probability clusters."[11]

Ever wary that he was overwhelming his human audience, or explaining too much, he added, "This material should not make you feel unimportant or insignificant. The framework is so woven that each . . . [consciousness] is dependent upon every other. The strength of one adds to the strength of all. The weakness of one weakens the whole. The energy of one recreates the whole. The striving of one increases the potentiality of everything that is, and this places great responsibility upon every consciousness."[12]

Indeed, this is the overriding message inherent in Seth's work, the staggering interconnectedness of all things. As a consequence, and once again echoing Bohm's notion of an underlying holographic order, Seth explained that we should amend our bias that we are somehow separate from the fabric of the whole. Each of us possesses a uniqueness in that we are separate and individual focuses of consciousness, but each of us is also part of a vast symbiosis, an infinitely interpenetrating network of dances within dances within dances. Thus, Seth conceded that he was both an extension of Roberts' own constellation of consciousness as well as an individual focus of consciousness unto himself, and that each of us is like an iceberg being, a pinpoint of self-awareness with roots and sinews extending through a far vaster symbiotic organization of intelligence of which we are not yet consciously aware.

Consciousness is in all things, said Seth, and thus we are different in degree but not in kind from all those other self-organized oases of life we recognize around us. Consequently, there is no ultimate fundamental spiritual difference between humanity and the creaturehood from which it has evolved. Indeed, like the physicist Dyson, Seth acknowledged that there is consciousness even in subatomic particles, although he stressed that the degree of consciousness manifested at this level of matter should not be thought of as possessing "human characteristics." Assuming a strikingly Prigoginian viewpoint, he suggested that it would be better to view these constituents of matter as possessing the "inclinations," "leanings," and "propensities," in short, the same "qualifications of being," that manifest more obviously in those organizations we recognize as living things.

The reason for this is so that "all probabilities are probed and experienced, and all possible universes [are] created" in this great dance of being we know of as existence.[13]

Bohm, Wheeler, Prigogine, and Dyson are not the only thinkers in this book whose thoughts agree with Seth's. Like Dawkins, he recognized that the information of our thoughts should be thought of as behaving very much like "viruses, for they are alive, always present, responsible, and possess their own kind of mobility."[14] Like Eccles, he asserted that the consciousness is separate from the brain, but is deeply "intertwined" with it, controlling it for the duration of physical evidence.[15] Like Sheldrake, he acknowledged that genes and chromosomes do indeed contain within them the coded information necessary for physical existence, but asserted that this information is conveyed "in another dimension entirely" and is "impressed" upon them at the time that they are materially formed. And mirroring Hoyle's suggestion that some sort of future-to-past time signaling is sometimes involved in evolutionary advance, Seth asserted that a type of precognition is indeed occasioned in evolution so that a species can prepare itself in the present to take on those changes that will be necessary in the future.[16]

Seth also discussed a number of matters not yet pondered by science. For example, he asserted that consciousness ultimately has a quantum structure with its corresponding wave radiation, but stated that these ultrainfinitesimal quanta of consciousness are so small (millions could occupy the space of a single atom) that they are presently beyond the range of physical matter as we know it, again implying that they lie *beyond the quantum*.[17] Because they seem to form a part of what we've been calling the structure of the information picture proper, Seth warned that they should not be thought of as physical structures and that hence we will not be able to probe them with physical tools as we know them. However, like their vastly bulkier cousins, he noted that these quanta of consciousness are already endowed with quantum uncertainty, or the inherent unpredictability that Seth alleged allows for the "infinite patterns and fulfillments" one finds in the reality systems they comprise.[18]

Seth concluded that it is these quanta of consciousness that comprise the substance of all beings and things, from the matter-concentrated murmurings of self-awareness we call ourselves, to beings at Seth's level and beyond. As for what does lie beyond, Seth also had much to say. He confessed that the concept of God is tricky, for as he noted, "the concepts of God that you have, have gone hand-in-hand with the development of your consciousness. The ego, emerging, needed to feel its dominance and control, and so it imagined a dominant god apart from nature. Often nations acted as group egos—each with its own god-picturing, its own concepts of power. Whenever a tribe or a group or a nation decided to embark upon a war, it always used the concept of its god to lead it on. The god concept then was an aid, and an important one, to man's emerging ego."[19]

This is not to say that there are no levels of conscious organization beyond Seth. Seth admitted that he too has his own Seth, an organization of intelligence as far in advance to him as he is to us. And beyond this, he asserted, are "complexities that are truly astounding, intelligences that operate in what I suppose you would call a gestalt fashion, building blocks of vitalities of truly unbelievable maturity, awareness, and comprehension. These are the near ultimate (as I understand such things)."[20]

As for his purpose in telling us all of this, Seth's summary of his reasons were as simple as they were eloquent. His goal was to awaken us to the fact that we live in a meaning universe in more ways than one. Or as he put it, "I am telling you that you are not a cosmic bag of bones and flesh, thrown together through some mixture of chemicals and elements. I am telling you that your consciousness is not some fiery product, formed merely accidentally through the interworkings of chemical components. You are not a forsaken offshoot of physical matter, nor is your consciousness meant to vanish like a puff of smoke."[21] He concluded, "[so] forget the cringing selves that you sometimes are and remember, instead, the magic essence of your own being that sings even now through your fingertips. That is the reality which you are seeking. Experience it fully."[22]

# 9

# Why Is Science Afraid of the Paranormal?

> When man first began modeling the universe around him, paranormal functioning was gracefully accepted as one of the phenomena to be accounted for, and therefore occupied an important place in religion and philosophy. However, as models of the universe were built to explain certain mechanical aspects of our environment, the phenomenon of paranormal functioning was found difficult to assimilate into the mainstream exploration. It therefore became suspect, a symbol of the anxiety humankind felt about the inadequacy of its model-building efforts. The tension culminated in the materialistically oriented concepts of early mechanistic science whose claim to fame was its apparent independence from subjective factors. Now that our modern scientific paradigm has strong roots in our culture, and it is recognized that the inclusion of observable subjective factors will not result in the destruction of all that has been gained . . . perhaps our place in the universe is . . . secure enough that we can begin to take another look at a piece of ourselves that we have long attempted to ignore. Perhaps humankind has matured.
>
> —RUSSELL TARG AND HAROLD PUTHOFF,
> *Mind-Reach*

Now, as we come to the end of our assessment of various and recent scientific viewpoints on some of the great metaphysical questions of all time, a few last important points need to be made. To begin, it may seem in the panorama of exciting ideas we have covered that some sort of scientific consensus is being reached. This is definitely not the case. Throughout this book I have tried to stress that many of the ideas presented are extremely controversial, and the issues so complex and fraught with subtle difficulties of language that it is doubtful that any two researchers whose work has been covered in this book would agree down the line on everything.

This is not necessarily bad. It is often out of controversy and different ways of viewing things (fluctuations in the human collective that lead to bifurcation points) that come the most important new advances in understanding. All of this notwithstanding, there is a problem in science. Serious research in the paranormal is a relatively rare thing, and no great strides (aside from those of isolated researchers) are being taken to further our knowledge of some of the most profound and potentially most beneficial mysteries in our midst. Science is not properly dealing with some of the most staggering discoveries it has ever made.

Let us take, for example, the most recent findings in quantum physics. As we have seen, the Aspect experiment has brought us to what is no less than a breathtaking fork in the road in our understanding of physical reality, and yet, for the most part, the reaction in the scientific press has been amazingly low-key—indeed, smacking almost of disregard. And as we have seen, this is not because the philosophical implications of the experiment are unrecognized.

Why, then, aren't they stirring up more scientific interest? One reason is that many physicists simply aren't interested in the philosophical implications of their work. Time and again in my own conversations with scientists, the fervor with which they discussed the basic day-to-day operations of their work vanished when I asked them what the philosophical implications of their findings were. Some became annoyed, asserting that philosophy should not be part of the structure of science proper. Others were clearly just not interested in anything other than the nuts and bolts aspects of their work. The larger questions surrounding their studies just weren't their cup of tea. Or as John Polkinghorne of the Department of Applied Mathematics and Theoretical Physics at Cambridge University put it recently, "Your average quantum mechanic is about as philosophically minded as your average garage mechanic."[1]

Another reason, and an even more serious problem, is that science is not value free. Science is so vociferous about its alleged stance of open inquiry, and so impressive in so many of its remarkable achievements, that most of us tend to forget that it is made up of human individuals with as many human foibles and blindnesses as the rest of us. This fact becomes most insidious when we ourselves do not have the expertise to judge when a scientist (whose reputation and opinion we otherwise have every reason to respect) is conveying to us a reasonable approximation of the truth or merely one of his or her own particular blindnesses.

As an illustration of all this, a few years back I was at a dinner party at which there were a well-known physicist, a well-known parapsychologist, and a well-known actress. The actress had just completed the filming of a seriously intended movie with a paranormal subject, and after she finished describing a psychic experience of her own she asked the physicist why science was not studying such things more earnestly. The physicist replied that if there was the slightest shred of evidence in favor of the paranormal, science would be pouncing on it. But, he related, there simply was no such evidence.

The actress, having no reason to doubt the physicist's expertise in the matter, was about to accept his dictum when the parapsychologist spoke up and vehemently asserted that the physicist's remark simply wasn't true. He explained that there was indeed plenty of evidence to demonstrate the va-

lidity of paranormal functioning and that it was largely ignored by both the physicist as well as the scientific
establishment in general. As the conversation continued, the
prejudice inherent in what the physicist considered evidence
of paranormal functioning became apparent, and the actress
realized that it wasn't as closed and shut a case as the physicist had previously implied.

Many scientists are so convinced that paranormal functioning does not exist that no amount of evidence, no matter
how substantiated or credible, will ever persuade them that
it does. For example, Puthoff and Targ report that in sub-
mitting one article on remote viewing, one response they
received from an "expert" consulted by an editor at the
periodical in question, was, "This is the kind of thing that I
would not believe in even if it existed."[2]

I myself have often been told the same thing by various
scientists. With equal frequency I have witnessed otherwise
eminent researchers expressing adamant opinions on subjects or experiments of which they have no knowledge. For
example, more than once in my discussions with various
scientists I would ask their opinion of the work of one or
more of the researchers mentioned in this book and be told
with no small amount of passion that it was "quackery."
When I inquired why they felt this way, sometimes I would
be given reasonable criticisms, and these I have tried to include in the book. However, sometimes I would be told that
it was quackery because it was "not science." And when I
asked why it was not science, I would be told "because it's
nonsense," and so on, in a circular argument whose ultimate lack of substance revealed that the scientist so fervently
espousing an opinion really had no specific knowledge of
the researcher's work.

Another fact, symptomatic of the curious and occasionally destructively inappropriate zeal with which some individuals take up against serious research in the paranormal,
concerns the much ballyhooed accounts of professional ma-

gicians who, pretending to be psychics, set out to fool certain researchers simply to prove that they are vulnerable to deceit. It is true that the paranormal is rife with an element of charlatanism, and there is no doubting that used properly the information provided by professional magicians is a valuable factor in separating the wheat from the chaff, as it were, in paranormal research.

But what does it say about us as a culture if we consider it meaningful that a well-meaning scientist under extraordinary circumstances can be fooled in any given and isolated incident? Certainly it may be argued that purposeful deceit may be a slightly more significant factor in paranormal research than in some other scientific endeavors, but as William Broad and Nicholas Wade have shown in their recent and enlightening book *Betrayers of the Truth,* fraud and deception have played a destructive role in numerous other fields of scientific research as well. How would we, or the press, respond if a professional magician announced that he had faked data in cancer research and fooled an eminent researcher? Would we consider it a service or a hindrance to the advancement of science? The fact that such events are greeted with relative complacency when it comes to paranormal research is once again evidence of the prejudice we have as a culture against the legitimacy of such research. Is this really what we want science to be like? Do we really want what we so cavalierly refer to as "an air of open inquiry" to reach the point where the prejudice of a few individuals with a flare for publicity are able to decide for us, and before the proper experimentation has been done, what is proper subject matter for scientific research and what is not?

Why is science so afraid of the paranormal? First of all, it is important to point out that this is not true of all scientists. Indeed, in a survey published in the early 1970s in the British publication *New Scientist*, a survey of 1,500 respondents (the majority of whom were working scientists and technologists), 67 percent considered ESP to be an established fact or likely possibility, and 88 percent acknowledged that the investigation of ESP was a legitimate scientific undertaking.[3]

Thus, the problem is not that a significant number of scientists aren't as open to the idea of paranormal functioning as the rest of the general public seems to be, but more that something about the structure of science prohibits it from being a subject fully worthy of serious study. As for what that something is, a short conversation with any physicist who has ventured into the taboo territory of the paranormal will reveal that science is a complex and brittle web of peerage, in which to go against anything that is not fully sanctioned by the network can be as risky and intimidating as announcing that the emperor has no clothes.

In a recent interview, physicist Peter A. Carruthers, head of the theoretical division of the Los Alamos National Laboratory, admitted that it was near craziness for him to brave the approbation of his peers and commit his thoughts on a possible physical mechanism for ESP in a technical paper a decade ago. Today, however, he feels that he may have been too cautious in the past and that, for that reason, some of his best ideas lie unpublished in his notebooks. Carruthers stated, "One shouldn't have a locked mind about these illicit borderlands of science. It's a mistake to think that because things aren't well explicated, or the evidence isn't clean, that they're manifestly false. They just aren't yet admitted to what is known as science."[4]

The problem goes deeper, however, than just fear of peer disapproval. I think that it also has a great deal to do with what I've been calling the Edge of the Map Syndrome. A quick glance at any history book will reveal that it has always been the norm, not the exception, in science always to strive to tie our current understandings of the world up into a neat package and view anything that lies outside that package with contempt and ridicule. Every new world has

been disparaged before it was embraced. When van Leeu-
wenhoek, the inventor of the modern microscope, tried to
tell his fellow human beings that there were bacteria living
in the saliva in their mouths, the populace at large thought
he was out of his mind. When Freud tried to convince his
colleagues and the educated public that there was a portion
of their thoughts of which they were unconscious, his ideas
more often than not became the subject of amused chatter.

It seems that we do not like our understanding of things
to have blurry edges. In fact, we get downright heated if
someone tells us that they do. It is something deep, perhaps
primordial—the same primal necessity that drove the first
protoplasmic stirrings of life in Earth's ancient seas to understand that there was survival value in establishing clearly
defined borders around that which it biochemically deter-
mined as self.

Whatever the cause, there is a deep and abiding need in
science to feel that it has it all figured out. Physicist Sir
Hermann Bondi of the University of London has called this
the "lure of completeness."[5] Which is why perhaps so many
of the great thinkers of our past, after taking human understanding further than it had ever been before, always
seemed to stop as if they had reached an invisible embank-
ment, and for all their genius could go no further. Einstein,
whose thoughts roamed freely in the initially intimidating
wilderness of curved space and relative time, after formulating his theory of relativity never wanted to take it to its
logical conclusion, and for the remainder of his life he remained supremely disinterested in black holes.

This is perhaps why so many of today's great thinkers,
who are able to accept so readily that the act of observation
is the warp and weft of things, have similarly stopped and
wish to ponder no further the potentialities or paranormal
capabilities of thought.

We have come so far and we know so much. Is it not
time that we abandon our fear of paradigm shift in science?

Should we not more readily embrace the fact that all great understandings will sooner or later be subsumed by further understandings, and that this is not a bad thing? Newton's understanding of planetary motion did not die or cease to have its function when Einstein's understanding of the relativity of space-time took its place. And Einstein's understanding will not die or cease to have its function when further understandings take its place. For all are part of the great symbiosis of thought, and all theories will ultimately be subsumed and incorporated just as all organismic innovations are ultimately subsumed and incorporated in the inexorable march of evolutionary advance.

Is it not time, then, that we recognize that, like information, truth too is an organic thing, always growing, always changing? And instead of striving for some ultimate truth in our scientific theories, shouldn't we judge them only in terms of how useful they are as tools? I remain convinced that there are laws of physics yet undiscovered, for I will never forget the sound of the poltergeist striking the window as I gazed into the darkness beyond. The human race has reached a threshold of wisdom in which it can at long last abandon the lure of completeness and recognize that whatever form they take, there will always be new vistas to be discovered in science, and new worlds awaiting us beyond the quantum.

# NOTES

## INTRODUCTION

1. Fritz Rohrlich, "Facing Quantum Mechanical Reality," *Science* 221, no. 4,617 (September 23, 1983), p. 1,251.

2. Basil Hiley, "Quantum Mechanics Passes the Test," *New Scientist*, January 6, 1983, p. 19.

3. Paul Davies, *Superforce: The Search for a Grand Unified Theory of Nature* (New York: Simon & Schuster, 1984), p. 47.

## 1

1. Davies, op. cit., p. 34.

2. Ibid.

3. Heinz Pagels, *The Cosmic Code* (New York: Simon & Schuster, 1982), p. 146.

4. Gerald Feinberg, *What is the World Made of?* (New York: Anchor Press, 1977), p. 132.

5. D.E. Thomsen, "Fractional Hall Effect by Electrons in Chorus," *Science News* (126, no. 8, August 25, 1984), p. 116.

6. Werner Heisenberg, *Physics and Philosophy* (New York: Harper & Row, 1962), p. 42.

7. A.P. French, *Einstein: A Centenary Volume* (Cambridge, Massachusetts: Harvard University Press, 1979), p. 276.

8. L. Rosenfeld, in *Proceedings of the Fourteenth Solvay Conference* (New York: Interscience, 1968), p. 232.

9. As quoted in Abraham Pais, *'Subtle is the Lord . . . The Science and the Life of Albert Einstein* (New York: Oxford University Press, 1982), p. 456.

10. Lee Smolin, "What is Quantum Mechanics Really About?" *New Scientist* (108, no. 1,479, October 24, 1985), p. 42.

11. John Gleidman, "Interview with Brian Josephson," *Omni* (4, no. 10, July 1982), p. 88.

12. D.E. Thomsen, "Holism and Particlism in Physics," *Science News* (129, no. 5, February 1, 1986), p. 70.

13. D.E. Thomsen, "Quanta at Large: 101 Things to do with Schrödinger's Cat," *Science News* (129, no. 6, February 8, 1986), p. 90.

14. Ibid.

15. Ibid.

16. Malcolm W. Browne, "Quantum Theory: Disturbing Questions Remain Unresolved," *The New York Times*, February 11, 1986, p. C6.

17. Davies, op. cit., p. 47.

18. Robert Temple, "David Bohm," *New Scientist*, November 11, 1982, p. 364.

2

1. David Bohm, "Hidden Variables and the Implicate Order," transcript of a talk given at Birkbeck College, University of London, January 1985, pp. 1–4.

2. Robert Temple, "David Bohm," *New Scientist*, November 11, 1982, p. 364.

3. Bohm, op. cit., p. 11.

4. Renée Weber, "Field Consciousness and Field Ethics," in Ken Wilbur *The Holographic Paradigm and Other Paradoxes* (Boston, Massachusetts: New Science Library, 1982), pp. 35–43. See also J. Krishnamurti and David Bohm, *The Ending of Time* (San Francisco: Harper & Row, 1985).

5. Temple, op. cit., p. 363.

6. John Gliedman, "Mind and Matter," *Science Digest*, March 1983, p. 70.

7. David Bohm, *Wholeness and the Implicate Order*, (London: Routledge & Kegan Paul, 1981), p. 134.

8. Gliedman, op. cit., p. 72.

9. Bohm, *Wholeness and the Implicate Order*, p. 145–7.

10. Gliedman, op. cit., p. 68.

11. Bohm, "Hidden Variables and the Implicate Order," p. 13.

12. Bohm, op. cit., p. 198.

13. Ibid., p. 199.

14. See Karl Pribram, *Languages of the Brain*, ed. G. Globus et al. (New York: Plenum, 1971); Karl Pribram, *Consciousness and the Brain* (New York: Plenum, 1976).

15. Wiktor Osiatyński, *Contrasts: Soviet and American Thinkers Discuss the Future* (New York: Macmillan, 1984), pp. 70–73.

16. Gliedman, op. cit., p. 72.

17. David Bohm and Renée Weber, "The Physicist and the Mystic—Is a Dialogue Between Them Possible?" in Ken Wilbur, op. cit., p. 196.

18. Bohm, *Wholeness and the Implicate Order*, p. 209.

19. Ibid., p. 213.

20. Ibid., p. 185.

21. David Bohm and Renée Weber, "Nature as Creativity," *ReVision* (5, no. 2, Fall 1982), p. 40.

22. Temple, op. cit., p. 365.

23. Gliedman, op. cit., p. 115.

3

1. Wolff, as quoted in Rupert Sheldrake, *A New Science of Life: The Hypothesis of Formative Causation* (London: Blond & Briggs, 1981), p. 20.

2. W. McDougall, "An experiment for the testing of the hypothesis of Lamarck," *British Journal of Psychology* 17 (1927), pp. 267–304; W. McDougall, "Second report on a Lamarckian experiment," ibid. 20 (1930), pp. 201–18; W. McDougall, "Fourth report on a Lamarckian experiment," ibid. 28 (1938), pp. 321–45.

3. Daniel Drasin, "Rupert Sheldrake, Ph.D.," *New Realities* (5, nos. 5 & 6, December 1983), p. 12.

4. David Bohm and Renée Weber, "Nature as Creativity," *ReVision* 5, no. 2 (Fall 1982), p. 35.

5. Rupert Sheldrake and David Bohm, "Morphogenetic Fields and the Implicate Order, *ReVision* 5, no. 2 (Fall 1982), p. 44.

6. I advanced a similar hypothesis in a previous book, *Mysticism and the New Physics* (New York: Bantam, 1980).

7. W. Harman, B. O'Regan, and Barbara McNeill, "Testing the Morphogenetic Field Hypothesis," *Investigations: A Bulletin of the Human Consciousness Research Program* (Sausalito, California: Institute of Noetic Sciences, 1983), p. 3.

8. Alan Holden and Phylis Singer, *Crystals and Crystal Growing* (London: Heinemann, 1961).

9. Lyall Watson, *Lifetide* (New York: Bantam, 1980), p. 147.

10. Rupert Sheldrake, *New Science of Life* (Los Angeles: J.P. Tarcher, 1981), p. 168.

11. Drasin, op. cit., p. 13.

12. Science Report, "Japanese Losing IQ Lead Over Americans," the *Times* (London), March 1, 1983.

13. John Gliedman, "Beyond the Brain's Boundaries," *Science Digest* 91, no. 2 (February 1983), p. 98.

14. Ibid.

15. Brian Goodwin, "Review: A New Science of Life," *New Scientist*, July 16, 1981, p. 164.

16. Drasin, op. cit., p. 11.

## 4

1. Anthony Smith, *The Mind* (New York: Viking Press, 1984), p. 230.

2. Roger Lewin, "Is Your Brain Really Necessary?" *Science* 210 (December 1980), p. 1,232.

3. Smith, op. cit., p. 230.

4. Lewin, op. cit.

5. Ibid.

6. Ibid., p. 1,233.

7. Ibid.

8. Daniel C. Dennett, *Brainstorms* (Cambridge, Massachusetts: M.I.T. Press, 1981), p. xiii.

9. Grey W. Walter, *The Living Brain* (New York: W. W. Norton, 1953), p. 251.

10. Daniel C. Dennett, "What Is It Like To Be Me?" *New Scientist*, September 24, 1981, p. 806.

11. Ibid.

12. Jerry A. Fodor, "The Mind-Body Problem," *Scientific American*, January 1981, p. 114.

13. John Gliedman, "Scientists in Search of a Soul," *Science Digest* 90, no. 70 (July 1982), p. 78.

14. Tom Kovach, "Out-of-Body Survey," *Omni* 4, no. 11 (August 1982), p. 94.

15. Ibid.

16. Michael B. Sabom, *Recollections of Death* (New York: Harper & Row, 1982), pp. 84–91.

17. Ibid., p. 91.

18. Ibid., p. 57.

19. Ibid., p. 183–84.

20. Fred Alan Wolf, *Star Wave: Mind, Consciousness, and Quantum Physics,* (New York: Macmillan, 1984), p. 134.

21. Douglas R. Hofstadter and Daniel C. Dennett, *The Mind's I* (New York: Basic Books, 1981), pp. 195–96.

22. Ibid.

23. Sir John Eccles and Daniel N. Robinson, *The Wonder of Being Human,* (New York: Macmillan, 1984), p. 156.

24. Ibid., p. 160.

25. Erich Harth, *Windows on the Mind* (New York: William Morrow, 1983), p. 75.

26. Eccles and Robinson, op. cit., p. 158.

27. Ibid., p. 162.

28. Ibid., p. 160.

29. Gliedman, op. cit., p. 76.

30. George A. Miller, "When We Think What Thinks?" *New York Times Book Review,* August 26, 1984, p. 22.

# 5

1. Heinz R. Pagels, ed., *Computer Culture: The Scientific, Intellectual, and Social Impact of the Computer, Annals of the New York Academy of Sciences,* vol. 426 (New York, 1984), p. 159.

2. Gregory Bateson, *Mind and Nature* (New York: Bantam Books, 1980), p. 12.

3. Gregory Bateson, *Steps to an Ecology of Mind* (New York: Ballantine Books, 1972), p. 488.

4. Bateson, *Mind and Nature,* p. 8.

5. Lyall Watson, *Supernature* (New York: Bantam Books, 1974), p. 65.

6. Edward O. Wilson, *Sociobiology* (Cambridge, Massachusetts: Harvard University Press, 1975), p. 60.

7. Ibid.

8. Ann Finkbeiner, "How Did Language Begin?" *Science 84,* (May 1984), p. 26; See also Lewis Thomas, "One Man's Candidates for the Wonders of the World," *New York Times* (June 7, 1983), p. C1.

9. Finkbeiner, op. cit.

10. "Research Roundup," *Science Digest* (92, no. 6, June 1984), p. 20.

11. Lorus and Margery Milne, and Franklin Russell, *The Secret Life of Animals* (New York: E. P. Dutton, 1975), p. 38.

12. Lynn Margulis, *Symbiosis in Cell Evolution* (San Francisco: W. H. Freeman, 1981), pp. 186–189.

13. Milne, op. cit., p. 54.

14. Michael Lemonick, "Machines with Living Parts," *Science Digest* (92, no. 2, February 1984), p. 26.

15. Fritjof Capra, "The Dance of Life," *Science Digest* (90, no. 4, April 1982), p. 32.

16. Ibid.

17. Lynn Margulis, "Symbiosis and Evolution," *Scientific American* (225, May 1971), pp. 48–57.

18. Robert Reid, "Genes Break the Rules in Mitochondria," *New Scientist* (December 11, 1980), pp. 721–723.

19. Margulis, *Symbiosis and Cell Evolution* (San Francisco: W. H. Freeman, 1981), pp. 242–243.

20. Richard Wolkomir, "The Wizard of Ooze," *Omni* (January 1985), p. 50.

21. Margulis, *Symbiosis and Cell Evolution*, pp. 242–243.

22. Wolkomir, op. cit.

23. Stephen Young, "The Dry Life," *New Scientist* (108, no. 1,480, October 31, 1985), p. 40.

24. James E. Lovelock, *Gaia: A New Look at Life on Earth* (New York: Oxford University Press, 1979).

25. Gerald Feinberg and Robert Shapiro, *Life Beyond Earth* (New York: William Morrow, 1980).

26. Ibid.

27. Mary Lukas, "The World According to Ilya Prigogine," *Quest/80* (4, no. 10, December 1980), p. 86.

28. Interview with Ilya Prigogine, *Omni* (8, no. 5, May 1983), p. 86.

29. Ibid., p. 88.

30. Ilya Prigogine and Isabelle Stengers, *Order Out of Chaos* (New York: Bantam Books, 1984), p. xv.

31. Ibid., p. xxi.

32. Interview with Ilya Prigogine, op. cit., p. 90.

33. Lukas, op. cit., p. 88.

34. Stefi Weisburd, "Halos of Stone," *Science News* (127, no. 4, January 19, 1985), p. 42.

35. Mitchell M. Waldrop, "The Large-Scale Structure of the Universe," *Science* (219, March 1983), p. 1,050.

36. Iris M. Owen with Margaret Sparrow, *Conjuring Up Philip* (New York: Harper & Row, 1976), p. 212.

37. Ibid., p. 71.

38. Daniel C. Dennett, *Brainstorms*, (Cambridge, Massachusetts: M.I.T. Press, 1981), p. 153.

6

1. Michael D. Lemonick, "Gravitational Lenses: Mirages from across the Universe," *Science Digest* (93, no. 4, April 1985), p. 58.

2. John Gliedman, "Turning Einstein Upside Down," *Science Digest* 92, no. 10 (October 1984), p. 96.

3. Ibid.

4. John Wheeler, "The Mystery and Message of the Quantum," lecture given to the American Physical Society, February 1, 1984, pp. 8–9.

5. Ibid., p. 4.

6. Gliedman, op. cit., p. 36.

7. Robert Wright, "The On-Off Universe," *The Sciences*, January/February 1985, p. 7.

8. Ibid.; see also Norman Margolus, "Physics-Like Models of Computation," *Physica 10D* (1984), pp. 81–95.

9. An analogy first suggested by Wright, op. cit.

10. David Bohm, *Wholeness and the Implicate Order* (London: Routledge & Kegan Paul 1981), p. 203.

11. Russell Targ and Harold Puthoff, *Mind-Reach: Scientists Look at Psychic Ability*, (New York, Delacorte Press, 1977), p. 51.

12. Ibid., p. 52.

13. WGBH Television Station, *Nova* transcript, "The Case of ESP," Boston, Massachusetts, January 17, 1984, p. 16.

14. Targ & Puthoff, op. cit., p. x.

15. WGBH, op. cit., p. 12.

16. Ibid., p. 22.

17. Ibid.

18. Loren Eiseley, *Coming of the Giant Wasps*, Audubon, 1975.

19. Lyall Watson, *Lifetide* (New York: Bantam Books, 1980), pp. 173–174.

20. Ibid., pp. 166–168.

21. Charles Darwin, *The Origin of Species* (New York, New American Library, 1964), p. 168.

22. Wright, op. cit., p. 8.

23. Ibid.

24. Ibid.

25. Ibid.

26. Wheeler, op. cit., p. 4.

27. Ibid., p. 7.

28. Gliedman, op. cit., p. 96.

29. Ibid.

30. Wheeler, op. cit., p. 14.

31. Editors, "Trees Talk to One Another, *Science Digest* 92, no. 1 (January 1984), p. 47.

32. Monitor, "Plants have Childhood Memories," *New Scientist* 97, no. 1,340 (January 13, 1983): 88.

33. Bayard Webster, "Are Clever Animals Actually Thinking?" *New York Times*, May 31, 1983, p. C1.

34. Ibid.

35. Freeman Dyson, *Disturbing the Universe* (New York: Harper & Row, 1979), p. 249.

36. Helmut Schmidt, PK Experiments with Animals as Subjects," *Journal of Parapsychology* 34 (1970): 255–61 (as quoted in Watson, op. cit., pp. 176–177).

## 7

1. John Maddox, "New Twist for the Anthropic Principle," *Nature* (307, February 2, 1984), p. 409.

2. Brandon Carter, "Large Number of Coincidences and the Anthropic Principle in Cosmology," in M. S. Longair, *Confrontation of Cosmological Theories with Observation* (Holland: Reidel, 1974), p. 242.

3. Paul Davies, "The Anthropic Principle," *Science Digest,* October 1983, p. 24.

4. Fred Hoyle, *The Intelligent Universe* (New York: Holt, Rinehart and Winston, 1984), p. 219.

5. John Wheeler, "Beyond the Black Hole," in Harry Woolf, *Some Strangeness in the Proportion* (Reading, Massachusetts: Addison-Wesley 1980), p. 359.

6. Heinz Pagels, "A Cozy Cosmology," *The Sciences,* March 1985, pp. 34–38.

7. Bernard Carr and Martin Rees, "The Anthropic Principle and the Structure of the Physical World," *Nature* 278 (April 12, 1979), p. 612.

8. Robert Jastrow, *God and the Astronomers* (New York: Warner Books, 1978), p. 137.

9. Heinz Pagels, *The Cosmic Code* (New York: Simon & Schuster, 1982): p. 179.

10. Paul Davies, "God and the New Physics," *New Scientist,* June 23, 1983, p. 874.

11. Paul Davies, "On Being Lowered into a Black Hole," *New Scientist,* January 14, 1982, pp. 75–78.

12. Harold Morowitz, "The Beauty of Mathematics," *Science 82* 3, no. 8 (October 1982), p. 26.

13. Albert Einstein, *Sidelights on Relativity,* trans. W. Perret and G. Jeffery (London: Methuen, 1922).

14. Eugene Wigner, "The Unreasonable Effectiveness of Mathematics in the Natural Sciences," *Communications on Pure and Applied Mathematics* 13 (New York: John Wiley and Sons, 1960).

15. John Tierney, "Quest for Order: S. Chandrasekhar Meditates on Black Holes, Blue Skies, and Scientific Creativity," *Science 82* 3, no. 7 (September 1982), p. 73.

16. Paul Davies, *God and the New Physics* (London: J. M. Dent & Sons, 1983), p. 189.

17. Ibid, p. 210.

18. David Osselton, "Making a Monkey of Shakespeare," *New Scientist* 104. no. 1,428 (November 1, 1984), p. 39.

19. Francis Crick, *Life Itself: Its Origin and Nature,* (New York: Simon & Schuster, 1981), p. 88.

20. Fred Hoyle, op. cit., p. 245.

21. Ibid., p. 235.

22 Paul Davies, "God and the New Physics," op. cit., p. 874.

23. Philip J. Davids and Reuben Hersh, *The Mathematical Experience* (Boston: Birkhauser, 1981), p. 53.

24. Ibid., p. 21.

25. Richard Dawkins, *The Selfish Gene,* (New York: Oxford University Press, 1978), p. 21.

26. Ibid., p. 207

## 8

1. Stuart Holroyd, *Alien Intelligence* (New York: Everest House, 1979), p. 213.

2. Jane Roberts, *The Seth Material*, (Englewood Cliffs, New Jersey: Prentice-Hall, 1970).

3. Jane Roberts, *Seth Speaks*, (New York: Bantam Books, 1972), p. xv.

4. Roberts, *The Seth Material*.

5. Roberts, *Seth Speaks*, p. 20.

6. Ibid., p. 20.

7. Ibid., p. 7.

8. Ibid., p. 21.

9. Ibid., p. 69.

10. Ibid., p. 265.

11. Jane Roberts, *The "Unknown" Reality: A Seth Book*, vol. 2 (Englewood Cliffs, New Jersey: Prentice-Hall, 1979), p. 370.

12. Roberts, Ibid., vol. 1, p. 60.

13. Ibid., p. 67.

14. Jane Roberts, *The Nature of Personal Reality* (New York: Bantam Books, 1978), p. 125.

15. Ibid., p. 103.

16. Jane Roberts, *The Nature of the Psyche* (New York: Bantam Books, 1984), p. 6.

17. Roberts, *The "Unknown" Reality*, vol. 1, p. 72.

18. Ibid., p. 66.

19. Ibid., p. 112.

20. Ibid., p. 61.

21. Roberts, *Seth Speaks*, p. 10.

22. Ibid., p. 486.

## 9

1. John Polkinghorne, *The Quantum World* (Hartow, Essex, England, Longman, 1984).

2. Russell Targ and Harold Puthoff, *Mind-Reach* (New York: Delacorte Press, 1977), p. 169.

3. Christopher Evans, "Parapsychology—What the Questionnaire Revealed," *New Scientist*, January 25, 1973, p. 209.

4. William J. Broad, "Tracing the Skeins of Matter," *New York Times Magazine*, May 6, 1984, p. 58.

5. Sir Hermann Bondi, "The Lure of Completeness," in Ronald Duncan and Miranda Weston-Smith, *The Encyclopedia of Ignorance* (New York: Pergamon Press, 1977), p. 5.

# INDEX